Praise for
Change Management that Sticks

'A change management book that tells it like it is. Tailor-made for change agents and packed with relatable stories and case-study examples.'

—**Dr Wesley Donahue**, author of *Building Leadership Competence*

'A game-changer and go-to book for anyone with skin in the game for leading effective and sustainable change adoption.'

—**Sue Morris**, Director, Sustaining Change

'Great tools and sound advice that will take you from stakeholder assessment through to end-user adoption.'

—**Anne Rainey**, Senior Change Manager

'Tells you the stuff the textbooks don't—the stuff you really need.'

—**Natalie Thomson**, Change Portfolio Lead

'Doesn't dwell on the theory but gets right down to how to deliver change in a way that rings true and guarantees everyone comes along for the ride for real results.'

—**Paul Fuge**, Consumer NZ Powerswitch Manager

CHANGE MANAGEMENT

that STICKS

CHANGE
MANAGEMENT

that
STICKS

A Practical, People-centred
Approach, for High Buy-in,
and Meaningful Results

Barb Grant

Published by Barb Grant—barbgrant.com
Publishing Consultant: Geoff Affleck, AuthorPreneur Publishing Inc.—geoffaffleck.com
Edited by Nina Shoroplova—ninashoroplova.ca
Book Interior and E-book Designer: Amit Dey—amitdey2528@gmail.com
Cover and text design by 100covers.com
Illustrations by Paige Clark, 'Change Cat' Copyright © Paige Clark, 2023
A catalogue record for this book is available from the National Library of New Zealand.

ISBN: 978-1-99-118570-9 (paperback)
ISBN: 978-1-99-118571-6 (ebook)
ISBN: 978-1-99-118572-3 (audiobook)

BUS103000 BUSINESS & ECONOMICS / Organizational Development
BUS085000 BUSINESS & ECONOMICS / Organizational Behavior
BUS075000 BUSINESS & ECONOMICS / Consulting

To my father,
who taught me to be curious, to have courage,
and to always give a toss.

Change can be tangly, like a big
ball of yarn... but wait!

Change Cat is here to save the day!

Table of Contents

Introduction

'
've distilled my thirty years of change management experience into this book. It's a book of practical approaches, tools, techniques, and tactics. It's a conversation, packed with case study examples to bring concepts to life and show how they're applied.

I've written it because every year, thousands of business change projects are implemented. Few of them, however, have the change they deliver highly adopted by the people they are delivered to.[1] This is so common that it's almost become an accepted shortfall of project delivery. As if it's inevitable that people won't generally adopt a new change. This book is written on the basis that **this isn't true**. This book is written on the basis that the need to get the change adopted is the number one imperative to claim any kind of genuine success. This book is all about how to make the change stick! And thereby ensure that business organisations are more effective, profitable, and successful as they move forward.

Most books on the topic of change management are textbooks. They are dense, large, and often extremely academic. Most of them are highly methodological. They are also a dry read. This book is different. This book is written as a conversation between me and you. A practical conversation about the real things that count. One that covers when, why, and how to do these real things to ensure that a business change sticks. This book is one change manager talking to another change manager. It's a conversation about what you'll most likely encounter and what you should do about it to deliver meaningful change. That is change that doesn't just deliver shiny tech that nobody uses to sit idly on desktops. Or new policy in digital folders that no one ever opens or implements. It's about adopted change that sticks, matters, and deeply informs the day-to-day experiences of users. It's change that contributes to outcomes and realises benefits.

This book doesn't talk generally about change management. It's not the hundred-and-fifty-thousand-foot view, and it's not theoretical. It's written to help you break through the barriers to make change stick in practical ways that work. I know, because I've been using these techniques for thirty years as a change manager with national clients. These are the 'keepers'. They're the approaches, templates, and techniques I come back to time and time again to get change to stick. When I talk about a new idea, I give a practical example of what I mean and how to apply it. The book isn't for the academic. It's for the 'person in the arena'.[2] That's where change happens. It's for you, if you're a change manager, or a person helping others through change, but with a different job title. Most of all, it's about getting to the heart of change. To do that, you must pinpoint what really motivates people to embrace change. Then you have to do things in the right way and at the right time to grow and sustain that motivation. This is how you deliver change management that sticks.

Who is this book for?

This book is for you if you have 'change manager' as your job title. But it's also for you if you're someone who helps others through change but you have a different job title. You're also in the right place if you're a change leader who wants to get closer to the ground where the change really happens. A change leader who genuinely wants to understand the detailed road map to lead others successfully through change. And it's also definitely for you if you've led or been involved with business change, to see it all come to nothing at 'go-live'. No doubt that was because the change effort didn't get to the heart of the change and work out what would make it stick. It had not revealed and SOLD the change value to each person in the change process. Nor probably had it identified accurately what people wanted from the change to commit to it. This book will give you those answers.

You are also in the right place if you're a developing practitioner. One who really cares about delivering business change in a way that is authentic and respects people. Perhaps you've already been involved in a number of business change projects. Were you brought in way too late when the deliverables were a done deal and already poorly conceived and sold? Was there little remaining chance for high change adoption?

This book will help you understand how it could have looked different. Perhaps you've been involved in project change for a long time. But leaders may have a poor or immature view of what change management does and the value it brings. Then *change* is turned from a crucial collaborative partner to *an order taker*. One on an endless treadmill of communication and training. That satisfies leaders looking for lots of box ticking, but not much real benefit realisation. This book will give you reasons, tools, and the language to help position change management more effectively. The book is underpinned by a philosophy of change delivery that puts the change recipients at the heart of the endeavour. It will help you make the case for why it's not enough to just deliver widgets. And make the case for delivering real adoption. Where return on outcomes is maximised and disruption at go-live is minimised.

It's my goal to make this book as real, accessible, and practical as possible for you, the reader. This book, its structure, style, and content is a model for the message. I'm showing you 'how to do it' (change management) with every succinct sentence and every simple, practical 'no fuss' method. The content is a calling card. It shows how to deliver change management that is simple, appealing, and accessible. I can't cover every aspect of change practice. Nor can I cover everything I've learned about successful change delivery. But I can cover the essentials that will give you the most 'bang for the buck' to achieve high adoption that makes the change stick.

Who is Barb Grant?

There may be some things in the section above that piqued your interest. But maybe you're asking yourself, 'Okay, but who exactly is Barb Grant, and why should I listen to her?'

Well, first off, let me confess that I consider myself an accidental change manager. That's because for the first thirty years of my life I was focussed on being a professional singer. That journey is a book for another day.

In my early twenties, to finance my singing tuition, I started working in information management and learning practice. I started as a coder of e-learning (before it was trendy to call yourself 'an instructional designer'). Pretty soon, I was writing procedural user guides and reference manuals. I did process mapping and lots of learning development and facilitation. All this helped finance my singing lessons, but I also loved this work. It wasn't long before I was project-managing larger delivery pieces. I also developed service specifications, advised on system user interface design, and delivered communications. Lots and lots of communications.

At this stage, it dawned on me that my musical life and my life as a change delivery agent weren't so far apart. Singers are performers, entertainers. What they want above all else is to create moments. Moments of deep human connection. Connection between the composer, the song, the singer, and the audience. Moments that achieve a heightened instance of awareness. Moments that get to the heart of something authentic. Moments that remove barriers and bring people authentically together. Singers and change managers have this in common.

You can only truly understand people in the change process if you create authentic connection. It doesn't matter if the people are executive leaders, delivery partners, internal or external users, or interested onlookers. You must find a way to walk a mile in their shoes. You must speak directly to the joys and sorrows that inform their views of the world and their relationship to the change you're working to deliver. There's music in this dance of understanding. Music in the effort to understand the value to each individual of what's proposed. The ebb and flow of attraction and repulsion. Attraction to what's offered in the future state and repulsion from what must be let go from the present.

Change management is a performance sport of a kind. It's an act of commitment to future possibility and to those involved in the change process. A commitment to support them unfailingly through to the finish line. Like singing, it's an act of bravery and an act of deep humility. Singers are in service to the song and the artistic vision. Change managers are in service to the change outcome. They serve the recipients of the change and the vision of realised benefit. This is my credo.

The other essential connection is that emotions are at the heart of the singer's craft. And it's the same with change management. Change management is not a bloodless, clinical pursuit ruled by methodology and spreadsheets. The road to the heart of change is through emotion. Emotions must be acknowledged, understood, and respectfully influenced. Whether a change is adopted or not is primarily dependent on this alignment. This is an alignment to what those in the journey value and the emotions associated with those values. Adoption of any change will be high when the project outcomes are hooked into a movement toward gain and away from pain. This is what makes the change stick. But the hooks must be specific to each stakeholder. The trick is to get the right hook for the right stakeholder.

A singer would say that when you achieve this emotional connection with your audience, you have them 'eating out of the palm of your hand'. That means, they are in a state of receptivity. That receptive state is what every person in a change process must experience to feel empowered to choose change and stick with it.

Singers can't MAKE an audience 'like' them and be 'moved' by the performance. They can only set up conditions that lead the audience to 'say yes to the offer'. The audience chooses to be moved. Getting change adoption is the same. Change managers are in the business of setting up offers. They create conditions to make the offer of the future state more attractive than hanging on to the current state.

In the late nineties, I did a brief tour of duty in KPMG Consulting, a financial audit, tax, and advisory company. That's where I first heard the term 'change management'. There was a whole team of them in the organisation, which was quite rare for New Zealand at that time. I remember asking my boss what 'change management' meant and what did a change manager do? When he described it to me, I thought, isn't that what every businessperson working to achieve outcomes does?

From that time on, I began to move into change management practice, by being on the ground and DOING THE WORK, not theorising.

The first large-scale piece I worked on was the set-up of a new bank in New Zealand's postal service. I talk about that change journey and what I learned about change adoption from the experience in chapter 6.

Since that time, I've worked as the change lead on all manner of successful business projects. And in all kinds of industries and sectors; from banking to energy and telecommunications, I've done the work. I've worked on countless system implementations, from accounting software to human resources (HR), procurement and document management, information management and finance. I've worked on portal implementations for all manner of customer service and goods and service provisioning. I've worked on the start-up of new venture companies. Also, nationwide operating model end-to-end transformations of large-scale organisations. I've done call centre change implementations and countless operational system, process, and policy projects. In the last seven years, I've worked on very large-scale transformations in the government sector. Many of these were sector-wide, involving many government sectors and private entities.

The big pieces had internal user populations up to 10,500. The external populations have been in the multi hundred thousand, and sometimes million-plus, ranges. I've worked on pieces that were behavioural-, policy-, and process-led. I've worked on pieces in which the change leaders hadn't even considered behaviours as a thing!

Sometimes I've been brought in to fix what I'm told is a 'broken' team dynamic, only to find willing people doing their best with broken processes, crappy tech, and out-of-touch leadership.

One day I'll write another book called, 'How to Get Real about What the REAL Problem Is'.

Regardless of the scale, money spent, or outputs, one thing I've learned is that all successful change adoption starts with behaviours. What matters most is to understand those behaviours. Then to successfully influence the values and emotions driving those behaviours toward the change.

Money wise, I've worked on pieces that cost 250,000 in NZ dollars total to those in the multi-hundred-million-to-billion-dollar range. The tools and techniques and philosophies in this book still apply. They are regardless of size, user population, and cost. The fundamentals don't change.

As a change lead, I've always worked on the basis that my word is my bond. My strongest credential is my thirty-year track record of successful, highly adopted change delivery. That's brought me a steady stream of consulting work and a lot of repeat business.

Of course, not all of the projects I've worked on have been successful. I would venture that in those cases there was a big gap between what was delivered and what the real problem was. In those cases, my ability to influence leadership to understand this gap was limited, but I sure did learn a lot. Most importantly, out of all my experience, I've got the reputation of being someone who cares not only about getting it done, but about getting it done well. At times, that may mean I want to tell leaders what they *need* to hear and not what they *want* to hear. Learning how to do this well is part of the journey for the change manager. The language I use is carefully chosen to help you, the reader-cum-change-manager, position the more delicate messages! This book is the distillation of all my knowledge and experience in change management. I give you the thirty years of my wisdom of experience.

One final thing. Change managers are naturally curious people. It comes with the territory. If you've ever wondered how other change managers do it, then wonder no more. I share it all in this book.

Thirty years and more than forty successfully delivered projects is a lot of time to work out what works and what doesn't. It's also a lot of time to experience many of the common pitfalls and work out the best solutions to those pitfalls. These are all themed up and shared in this book. This is right down to nitty-gritty things, like how to create a meaningful stakeholder assessment. Or how to develop an outcomes-focussed and successful change impact assessment.

In this book, I share all of my favourite and successful tools, techniques, philosophies, and approaches.

What you'll learn in this book

Change management means many things to many people. To me, the essence is about creating deep human connections. The kind of authentic connections that motivate the permission to choose change. This book is fundamentally about how to create those connections. Then how to keep them aligned to project purpose.

Here's a breakdown of what's covered in each chapter, by sighting the magical beast known as 'the change', and how to navigate this book.

This short section describes how the concept of 'the change' is applied in the book. It describes the conventions used to help you understand how to apply the ideas presented.

Chapter 1—Values of the change manager. First, understand what you value, then align it to the change you support. In chapter 1, we'll define your own personal alignment with the change outcome. If you're going to live and breathe helping others to adopt something, it's best to have a clear sense of your own reasons to commit.

Chapter 2—Understand the stakeholders in the change and what they want. In chapter 2, we'll widen the frame to define all the stakeholders from the executive to the end users. We'll look at how to frame these stakeholders against their personal and group motivations and de-motivations. And how to use that understanding to create connections to the change purpose.

Chapter 3—Find the truth of the change. What is delivered that truly matters to each impacted group? Chapter 3 will help you craft those stakeholder motivations into clear outcome statements. We'll use the analogy of a Rubik's Cube to help understand which 'face of the change' your stakeholder is 'turned to'. This is what dictates what they will view as a movement toward gain and away from pain.

Chapter 4—The change impact assessment and 'What's in it for me?' Chapter 4 looks at how to craft and sell great 'what's in it for me' (WIIFM) statements. WIIFMs that work and WIIFMs that won't. Ones that will really motivate adoption and make the change stick.

Chapter 5—Build up from a base and keep it simple. Where to start your change effort and what to do. How to build a great change plan. Chapter 5 looks at how to take all of these great groundwork change deliverables and sequence them into a workable change approach. That's once you've fleshed out a great detailed change impact assessment to support your road map.

I give detailed guidance on how to develop the change impact assessment, down to what to put in each column and why. Your change impact assessment document is the 'one ring to rule them all' for a change manager. It's the most critical document. All your change delivery flows from this, so it's crucial to get it right. I also emphasise in this chapter when to focus on what and how much.

Many a change manager and project have come to grief focussing too much effort on the right thing but at the wrong time. This chapter and many others all strongly emphasise that 'Done is better than perfect.' That's if your focus is truly on the people and their change adoption, and not on the method and the deliverables!

Chapter 6—Black arts and dark ops. Understanding the basics of delivering successful behavioural change—the high-level playbook. Chapter 6 is about behavioural change. It's a longer chapter because I had a lot to say about this! Behaviours are motivated by belief systems and belief systems are based on emotions. Because dealing with emotions can be challenging, this is no doubt why I see so many change projects shy away from dealing with them. Some projects operate in total denial that they even exist! But people's behaviours, which are based on their emotions, comprise a most crucial piece.

This chapter explains how to get this part right and why it matters so much for change adoption. I give my detailed method of delivering successful behavioural change. This includes how to deliver specific team-based interventions. I also cover a range of real-life examples to illustrate behavioural change done right. Then behavioural change done wrong and the consequences.

Chapters 7 and 8 are troubleshooting chapters.

Chapter 7—Heading roadblocks off at the pass. Dealing with the barriers to change adoption. In chapter 7, I reframe the idea of 'change resistance' as 'change reaction'. I'll share two key ideas about how to work with the change reaction. These ideas are 'creative struggle' and 'the voice of the change'.

Chapter 8—Reframes and resets. How to rock the crunchy stuff. In chapter 8, the focus is on how to deliver bad news successfully. The trick is to be timely, clear, authentic, and still point toward the positive future state. I get very specific about how to craft good rescue messages that aren't self-serving. Ones that will get real *cut-through*— real penetration—with your audience. The sequence and mediums you use for these types of messages really matter too.

Chapter 9—Change readiness and success measurement. Making change matter. This chapter looks at how to conduct meaningful change-readiness activities. It steps through how to develop the three required business readiness assessments: baseline readiness, pre-go-live readiness, and post-go-live success measurement.

Chapter 10—Making the change stick. How to enable successful business handover. Chapter 10 is the final chapter. It covers the sometimes-fraught issue of finding the right business owners for the delivered change. That's not only the more 'obvious' owners of your change assets, but most importantly the owners of the realised change value.

I also talk in this final chapter about how savvy the change manager must be to organisational structure changes. The chapter lays out the common 'forces at play' in structural changes. It then covers how to navigate them to secure the best possible business owners. The notes section follows. This covers any references used in the book that you can look up for further information.

Finally, there's a glossary, where all of the idiomatic expressions and business related terms are explained chapter by chapter.

There's plenty in here for everyone, so let's get started ...

Sighting the magical beast 'the change', and how to navigate this book

Change managers frequently refer to 'the change'. By this, they mean the process of change management. But they also mean the things delivered out of a business change project. I follow this convention in this book. This is a peculiarity of the discipline of change management. *Change* IS both a verb and a noun. We can 'change seats' (verb) but we can also experience a 'change of heart' (noun). It depends on how the term is used.

In change management, the word 'change' is used as though it's simultaneously a noun AND a verb. A change manager will talk about 'the change' and mean both the transition the people are going through and 'the thing' being delivered. People 'go through the change', but they also 'receive the change'. It is a process, an event, and a key character in the unfolding story of delivery and adoption. This personifies the change. It's almost as if it is a magical beastie! 'The change' and the change manager are constant companions on the road to adoption of the change.

This book is about business change projects. Death and taxes are called the only certainties in life. I would add *change* to the list. It focuses on a subset of change and that's business change. This means any piece of new or enhanced change to a business environment that affects people. It could be a project or initiative, in which a current state is amended to a new, and not yet known, future state. It is for the people in the business who have to deliver that change. These people are usually people leaders or managers or sometimes professional business change managers. But they're also the 'Hey, you!' volun-told staff member.

Introducing...
the magical beast,
'the change'!

The book covers small, medium, and large-scale projects, and even programme change.

(It doesn't cover large-scale transformation programmes. That's a many-headed hydra for another time. It would be a longer book. In my experience, the subtitle of that book could be, 'The bigger they are, the harder they fall.' Or 'The more they cost, the less they deliver.')

The business change might be either a project or a 'business as usual' initiative. The tools, tips, and templates covered in this book will work well in both cases.

In this book I talk about the types of business change projects I've personally been involved in over the last thirty years. My strongest suits are communications (sometimes called *comms*), learning, engagement, process design, change readiness, and behavioural change. I am not an HR practitioner. I have worked on plenty of pieces that had significant HR components and organisational structure components. But I have always had HR specialists in my work stream to deliver any restructuring work.

Therefore, this book looks at business change delivery through the project and change lifecycles. And also, the end-to-end process model. These are in my wheelhouse. There's still plenty in this book for HR practitioners. There are chapters on values alignment and how to deal with project resets and reframes. There's also a chapter on how to understand stakeholders and their value propositions.

Finally, this book gives you lots of specific templates to use. Note that these are provided using an eighty / twenty approach. I can't cover every single instance of what COULD be included in, say, a change impact assessment or a change plan. Instead, I've focused on the key elements of each template, the elements I believe you MUST include. Those that will deliver 'the most bang for the buck'.

There are countless other items that you can add to your template. These will depend on the specifics of your change. What does it deliver? What are the outcomes and realised benefits? What are the forces acting upon it? What's the political climate? What does that do to the change perception? In other words, these templates are 'starters for ten'. What you choose to add or remove when you use them is as individual as the change you work on.

Here's the bread crumb trail. I hope it leads you to exciting new places and possibilities!

If you want to continue the conversation, go to www.barbgrant. com and sign up. Enter your name and best email to download a free workbook to use in conjunction with this book. There's lots of room to enter your own notes and ideas as you use this book on the job. Join my community to receive regular updates and access to free materials.

CHAPTER 1

Values of the Change Manager

Have you ever asked yourself how your personal values align with the business change you support? It's a good question to ask yourself. It's so much harder to support something that your personal values don't align with. Ideally, the projects you support will enhance, not compromise, your values. Most change managers care deeply about what motivates people to do what they do. But sometimes we forget to ask ourselves, 'Why do I do what I do?' We are no different from any other person participating in a change process. If the change agent isn't clear on their own stake in what's changing, they can become their own saboteur. Supporting the journey will start to feel like wading through quicksand.

First, understand what you value, then align it to the change you support

A lack of values alignment sets up a 'cognitive dissonance'. This means there's a gap between our own values and the goals and values of the change we seek to have adopted. The gap derails our ability to support the change effectively. We end up demoralised and disenfranchised.

When we work on changes that alienate us from our own core values, we're in the 'uncanny valley'. It's a chasm in which we are out of alignment from our true self. It's never a good idea to sell what you wouldn't buy.

It's crucial to know where you stand in relation to the change you're about to live and breathe. To illustrate, let's talk about my personal experience with professional burnout. I've worked as a business change and information manager for thirty years. This all went well until I got out of step with my personal values and the business change programme I led. I couldn't sleep, I worked crazy hours, my heart raced, my palms were sweaty. Worse, I got redder and redder (a red flag (pun intended) for extreme stress). Every day I would wake up and, with a sense of dread, realise it was a workday. I would lie there, trying to 'talk myself off the ledge'. I would tell myself today would be better, today HAD to be better. Needless to say, it wasn't. This went on for months. It became difficult to manage my thoughts and feelings. It became harder to convince myself I HAD to go to work. I hated the thought of all the people I would let down if I didn't go in. But the odds were against me. I had no access to senior leaders. That meant I couldn't build trust and confidence with the project sponsor. An army of external consultants were occupying key project positions. These consultants had their own agenda and spent much of their time undermining the independents (such as me). The organisation also had a real lack of experience delivering large-scale change. That meant not a lot of people knew what *good* looked like. They didn't know what they didn't know. But no one was asking.

Attempts to promote team culture and common purpose were inauthentic. The unsaid, but powerful, message of the programme culture was 'win at all costs—failure is not an option'. There was a huge disconnect between 'what I say and what I do' in what was modelled. Leaders can say, 'Bring me the issues; I'm open and transparent'.

But if the behaviour is the opposite, then everyone on the team knows it's NOT OKAY to say what needs to be said.

Sure, there were endless team days and team events. But organisational culture knew that 'Do what I say and don't ask questions' was the real message. Strong indicators like sky-high team turnover and long silences in meetings, where no one would venture an opinion, told the real story.

My personal values

It was when someone asked me why I was so red all the time that I realised I had to get out. I started seeing a career counsellor. She told me I needed to start by understanding my personal values. Then I needed to understand how big the gap was between those values and the work I was doing. At first, I was sceptical, but we proceeded. We used values cards in a pack, which I needed to sort down to the ones I felt most connected to and then cull them down to a final list.

My initial list was this:

- courage
- creativity
- empathy
- enlightenment
- freedom
- honesty
- intuition
- joy
- laughter
- play
- trust
- truth

In the second review I got it down to:

- courage
- creativity
- enlightenment
- honesty
- intuition
- love
- trust

That's my list, but it might ring some bells for you. There are many formal methods you can find online to assess your personal values. A google search on 'How do I understand my values?' will yield many results. There are two credible and informative references for this at the end of this book.[3]

To be an effective change enabler, you must first understand your personal values. Then make sure there is some alignment between your values and the values and goals of what you're enabling.

Here's an exercise to help you assess your personal values

Get a feel for your personal values. Read through the list of values below and select the ones that speak to you the loudest. You should end up with about ten max.

achievement	bravery	creativity
amusement	clarity	delight
appreciation	compassion	dependability
authenticity	competitiveness	devotion
balance	contentment	empathy

exhilaration	kindness	sensitivity
fairness	love	serenity
freedom	loyalty	service
happiness	lucidity	thoughtfulness
honesty	peacefulness	tolerance
honour	precision	toughness
humility	reliability	tranquillity
independence	resilience	trustworthiness
integrity	respect	truthfulness
intuition	responsiveness	understanding
joy	selflessness	willpower

Now revisit your list, and pair up the values you've selected that are most like each other. Then for each group of similar values, choose the one that is most meaningful for you. Discard the rest. For instance, if you selected *happiness, joy,* and *delight,* you could group these together. Then you could choose *joy* as the word that best captures the essence of those values for you. You want to get your list down to about six core values or fewer if you can.

Now that you have a sense of your core values, you want to ask yourself, 'How IS that for me?'

Any surprises? If there are, sit with them for a while. It can be helpful to reflect on where you feel those values came from. Who were the significant people in your life who gave you that code of core values? What were the life experiences that created them? How in alignment do you currently feel with those values?

In this book, we're applying these values to a business change you're working on in your professional career. It may also be helpful for you to look at how these values relate to your personal life. You could look at what they mean in terms of your health and social relationships for instance.

Your values and the business change values

Now, let's compare these values to the business change you're about to shepherd through to delivery. Let's see if the change aligns, or fails to align, with your personal values.

Here's a table to help you do this.

No.	Value	What it means for me in a work context	What it looks like right now in a work context	Aligned (Yes/No)
1				
2				
3				
4				
5				
6				

Exercise to determine how your business change aligns with your core values

In the table above

1. Write your short-list of six values in the second column.

2. Write a statement that describes what each value means to you in the third column.

3. Write a statement in the fourth column that describes how you can or can't apply this value in your current work assignment.

4. Score each row with a 'Y' for yes or 'N' for no in the fifth column.

5. Add up how many 'yes' and 'no' answers you have in the 'Aligned' column.

This could be an interesting exercise. Hopefully, it's not too confrontational! In my case it was super confrontational, but it helped me make the change I needed to make for both my professional and personal sanity.

Once you've got your list of values, relate it to what you're working on and see how many of your values align.

Out of alignment

The table below shows you how it looked for me. Heads up. This is a worst-case scenario for illustrative purposes only!

Hopefully, completing your own table yielded good news for you. If not, maybe it's still a good thing, right? Because, once we have this clarity, we have either renewed purpose or the opportunity to make a new choice.

In my case, the process helped me to understand that I was in a dire situation. There was complete misalignment between what I personally valued and the work I was doing. It gave me the clarity to stop dragging myself into a workplace and project I'd grown to hate.

When you work to enable change, you must be a cheerleader. That's why the value alignment matters so much. You are also a salesperson and a committed advocate for the change. Anything less and it will be hard to sustain your energy. Then if you keep 'running on empty', there can be significant personal cost. At the least, you'll become disenchanted with the work. It will be miserable and hard to sell the change successfully. People read lack of authenticity very fast.

No.	Value	What it means for me in a work context	What it looks like right now in a work context	Aligned (Yes/ No)
1	Enlighten-ment	I strongly value being a truth teller and I pride myself on the deep insights I can provide on the road ahead.	Don't have the ear of senior leaders. Not seen as someone in the 'inner-circle'. Can't influence the important decisions.	No
2	Love	I want to love what I do to know that the work I do matters. I love how it helps people to have a better working day and that I help people.	Hard to be loving in a fearful environment. Sycophancy is rewarded. Deep human connection isn't. In fact, it's feared.	No
3	Creativity	I want to do new things every day. I want to understand puzzles and problems. I want to find creative, innovative, cost-effective, and expedient ways to solve problems and help people.	Environment is dominated by the influence of other external parties. These parties have their own strong agendas. Others are actively discouraged from sharing their contribution.	No

4	Trust	I want to know that I am trusted, that the work I do is trusted, and that I can trust those I work with.	It's an environment of fear and toxicity. People who call things out are ostracised and terminated. There is no trust. There IS a lot of blame.	No
5	Courage	I want to do bold work. I don't want to settle for the status quo and the 'But we've always done it this way' excuses. I don't want to 'follow the book'. I want to do things that carry calculated risk but deliver massive opportunity.	Those that stick their head above the parapet here 'lose their head'. Outspoken and innovative ideas are actively discouraged. This has encouraged a 'yes' culture of conformity and low contribution.	No
6	Honesty	I want to say what needs to be said. I want to be valued and appreciated for it. I want to focus on the work and not on the personalities. I want to have that reciprocated. I want to have adult conversations with colleagues who are emotionally aware.	Don't have the mandate to say what needs to be said. This is viewed as 'not contributing appropriately'. It's not okay to be a truth teller, no matter how constructively this is offered.	No

What you're trying to 'sell' as the benefits of the change won't read as being authentic without your commitment.

You don't need to get a row of 'yes' answers in the 'Aligned' column for this to work. A few of your rows might be a 'no' for alignment. As long as you have at least one 'yes' that is a high priority for you, it could still work. So it's quite individual. What counts is that there are enough 'yes' alignments between your values and what you're working on. That's enough to sustain you through the tough times, because all change worth doing has tough times. This clarity is like a personal touchstone you can rub for inspiration anytime you need it. If you're working on a piece of change in which you have little choice in the matter, this process will at least grant you the clarity to know where your strongest personal alignment lies. In this case, do what you have to do until you're in a better position to choose projects with stronger personal values alignment.

Let's see how this might look for some common types of change projects you may end up working on.

Worked example—align your personal values to the change

In this example, the project will introduce automation to a claim assessment process. A back-office team does the claim assessment. Automated business rules will now assess client claims against the standard eligibility criteria. If there are no issues, the system will approve the claim and notify the customer. Where there are exceptions, a system task-and-alert is sent to a team member who will look into the application and fix the exception for approval or reject the claim.

Here's how the table might look in this case. The manager of the claims processing team is the change lead in this case. Their personal values are

- fairness
- resilience
- responsiveness, and
- loyalty.

Here's what their values table looked like related to the project described above.

No.	Value	What it means for me in a work context	What it looks like right now on the project/initiative	Aligned (Yes/ No)
1	Fairness	Straight-through claims can be automatically approved for a standard and fair result. More complex claims are identified for a much more in-depth assessment with less time pressure and a fairer outcome.	The project team is committed and wants to keep our team focussed on high value work. I'm the change lead. We need to work hard to make people understand why we're doing it. We need to be clear about how it offers more interesting work opportunities.	Yes
2	Resilience	The team has been doing the work under a lot of pressure, with too few team members having to look at every claim. This initiative will change this for the better.	We're starting to make headway with our people about how this will cut down the pressure to process claims quickly. We need to do a more thorough claim assessment when it's needed. There's an upskill opportunity to learn more about more complex claims.	Yes

3	Respon- siveness	My team and I have always been committed to being as responsive to our customers as possible before the work volume really slowed us down.	People are starting to get that this will help us all provide a faster and more accurate service for our customers.	Yes
4	Loyalty	I've been with this team a long time. They're important to me.	Redundancies may result from this change. But it looks like those who choose voluntary redundancy will cover it. That's a big relief. The real focus is to give our people more interesting work. This creates more development opportunities.	Yes

Now this is a pretty favourable table for values alignment, and it helps you get the idea. As a colleague of mine once commented, 'the grass is always browner.' This means it's likely that no matter what change piece you work on, some things will align well, and some won't. It's hard to get all the grass green. You must decide whether the areas of misalignment are discomforts you can live with or discomforts you can't. All grass is a bit brown in patches. It all depends on the brown you can live with and the brown you can't.

My personal example was a dire case. It served me as a call to action to get out. I did and moved on to a much more values-aligned project instead.

First, do your values assessment. Then you assess what gets a 'no' for alignment. Ask yourself for each one, 'Is this a deal breaker, or not?' If it's something you can live with, ask yourself how you're going to live with it. Describe that for yourself in a few sentences to make sure it's legit. Then think about what you can do to improve the odds of it being tolerable.

Think through if there's anything you could do to turn the deal breakers around. Is there a courageous conversation with a colleague that could improve the work relationship? Or it could be getting approval to have a courageous conversation! Is it worth it to you? Is the upside of taking that action superior to the negative consequence?

Nourishing or depleting your core strengths

If your alignment column at the end of this process doesn't look too good, there's another step. You should ask yourself whether those noes are depleting your strengths.

Until I worked with a career coach, I hadn't ever thought about this, but I sure as heck was feeling it!

If we keep using depleted strengths, they can become weaknesses. We draw from a dry well. My depleted strengths were in managing teams, mentoring, and team building. If you check in with your feelings, you will know when using a strength starts to deplete you: using the skill will start to drain your energy. Instead of looking forward to opportunities to use that skill you'll start to dread it. We move from a state of nourishment to a state of overwhelm. What used to energise us now exhausts us. You can't give and give from an already dry well. You will grow to resent the skills and talents you were once proud to celebrate. Then you start to lose your identity.

I had got to a state where I dreaded team meetings. Worse yet was a team member asking if I 'had a minute'! Oh, the dreaded minute! I should have seen the red flags long before this. But when we run on empty in a high stress environment, a certain doggedness sets in. That's another sign to watch for.

Run a quick exercise to brainstorm your strengths.

Ask yourself the following questions to identify your strengths

1. What do you love to do and why?
2. What do you hate to do and why?
3. What were you doing when you were happiest?
4. Why did doing this make you happy?
5. Picture yourself in your ideal future state. What does it look like? What are you doing? Why is that ideal to you?

Based on your answers to the questions above, write down a list of five or more strengths. Now take a look at your values-aligned-with-the-project table. Ask yourself if those strengths are being nourished or depleted. Which ones are being depleted? Why is that and what could you do about it?

It's worth feeling around for solutions. That's if you have a connection to the work and the outcomes. Watch if none of those factors score as a positive for you. That's a red flag that means it's time to ask yourself whether this one is 'still the go' or not.

Summary

That's chapter 1 done. Now that you've finished this chapter you should have a clear idea of the following:

1. How important it is to align your personal values with the business change.
2. What your core values are.
3. How your values relate to the business change initiative you're working on.

4. Whether the business change supports your core values or not.

5. How to improve the relationship between your core values and the project change, and whether the effort is worthwhile.

6. Your core strengths. Whether the work is nourishing your core skills or depleting them.

The core message of this chapter is that to support business change you need a clear picture of your own commitment to the change journey. You need to know if it enhances or inhibits your personal values. When values align, it's easier to commit to enabling the change. Then it's easier to sustain the effort to get the change to stick. This means the likelihood that you can assist in getting to high change adoption is much greater.

In the next chapter, we look at who is playing in the sandpit and how to understand what they want.

CHAPTER 2

Understand the Stakeholders in the Change and What they Want

There are two things you must understand to sell your business change initiative. One is who you're selling it to. Two is what they want from it. There are always obvious stakeholders, often those who will use what's delivered and those who asked for it. But, for the 60 to 70 percent of obvious stakeholders, there are always the less obvious. Forgetting these players is the reality check that will bite you in the butt when you try to deliver the change.

I once worked on a support project in the first stage of a large-scale transformation. The primary audience of 'people who pay the government fees' was quickly identified. There was a lot of focus on the support this group would need to transition successfully. This change support related to newly renovated processes, policies, system, and legislative rules around correct fees payment and the timing of payments. It also included a lot of mindset change.

But another important group didn't get identified. They were kind of there, but 'lumped in' with this primary category of 'people who pay the government fees'. This group comprised the agents who manage the payment of these owed fees on behalf of clients. The unique nature of these agents was not understood at first. They couldn't just be lumped in with 'people who pay government fees'. This group had significantly different needs. Their needs weren't anticipated or defined in terms of what was unique about them. That meant there was a tsunami wave of issues at go-live.

These agents expressed their frustration at the following:

- The system functions they couldn't access and still needed.

- The system functions they did have access to but hadn't had effective training on.

- The missing processes and business rules that linked them into the new operational flow.

- Their lack of understanding of why the change had been made and what the advantages to them were of adopting it.

- How they didn't understand what they had to do differently, the different conversations they now needed to have with their existing clients, and the conversations they needed to have to attract new clients.

The bullet points above cover all the classics. In this case, these points had to be retroactively addressed in great haste. That's not ideal. This is what happens if and when key stakeholders and their specific needs aren't identified and addressed early. It's crucial to get the stakeholder groupings right.

Therefore, it's good to have a method to identify ALL stakeholders. You need a map to contextualise what they want and when. The 'how to meet their needs' part will come in chapter 5, when we cover how to develop a great change plan.

Change Cat knew... it was the stakeholder you miss who'll bite you in the butt at project go live!

Four groups of stakeholders

This chapter is a primer to help you understand your stakeholders. It groups them up into broad categories with common traits. The first important actor in the change is, of course, you. You can't help all the folks unless you understand your own why. That was covered in chapter 1. What are YOU getting out of being part of this change? There's a wage or salary, of course, but what's the added value for you beyond your pay cheque? After reading chapter 1, you should know the answer to this question. It must be meaningful enough that you're committed for the long haul.

Let's look at the rest of the picture of who's in the change with you.

You can group stakeholders into four broad categories. The categories are initiators, partners, recipients, and interested onlookers. The first group, and arguably the trickiest to manage, are your change initiators. Big projects with big budgets are more politically charged. That means, the more complex are the perceptions (optics) of the change for this group. Higher stakes mean more pressure and often more intense emotional responses from leadership.

Let's look at these four groups in turn.

Group 1. Change initiators

These groups are 'on top of' the change process; they are the ones who trigger the change process. They are the board, the executives, and other organisational senior leaders such as general managers, directors, operational, strategic or functional managers, and deputy chief executives. Sometimes there are ministers and other senior political party officials. Often other public servants are in the mix. Sometimes there are regulators, legislators, and other compliance-based authorities.

Group 2. Change partners

These groups work 'on' the change; they are the ones who assist to design, develop, and deliver the change. These are internal and external subject matter experts, vendors, lobby groups, media, unions, and sometimes the general public.

Group 3. Change recipients

This group are 'in' the change process; they receive and use the change. Unlike the group above, they 'receive' the change when it's delivered. This group are often described generally as users, consumers, or clients.

Group 4. Interested onlookers

These are the other groups, both inside the organisation and outside it, who aren't directly impacted by the change but are invested in the outcome. This group is the rest of the organisation not directly impacted by the specific change. It also includes other partners or similar agencies or bodies who work in the same industry or sector.

Subcontracting parties to an organisation can be in here, as well as competitors, media, and the general public.

These are the four broad categories of stakeholder. The statements above describe their orientation to the change, or how they are 'turned toward the change'.

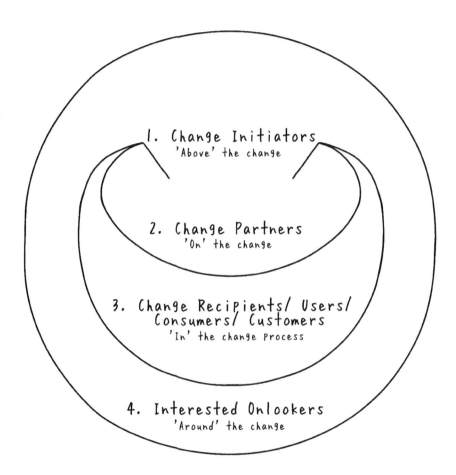

Now let's look at the table below, which highlights what these groups usually want in any change.

Group 1—Change Initiators—what they want and don't want

Stakeholder type	Do want from the change	Don't want from the change
Ministers and other political officials	Respect from other ministers and the prime minister. Positive media coverage. Realisation of key political agendas (that got them the job). Positive press coverage. Voter confidence.	Embarrassment. Hostile scrutiny. Critical articles and other negative publicity about the company. Disruption to business continuity. Ammunition for the opposition.
Boards	Delivery on the board's strategic plan. Kudos from peers and public. Positive media coverage about how the board is making a positive difference and turning the enterprise around. Cost reductions, increase in profits, return of increased shareholder valuer.	Embarrassment. Hostile scrutiny. Critical articles and other negative publicity about the company. Disruption to business continuity. Challenges to the board's credibility and authority.
Executives	Delivery on the executive's strategic plan.	Embarrassment.

	Kudos from the board, peers, the organisation, and the public. Approval of staff. Increased chance of promotion. Positive performance review. Positive publicity.	Miss and/or expose holes in the strategic plan. Fail to deliver strategic outcomes. Board censure. Public censure. Reputational risk (personal and organisational). Ridicule of colleagues and staff.
General managers; directors; operational, strategic or functional managers; deputy chief executives	Outstanding performance rating on their performance review. Respect and approval of direct manager. Respect of executives. Respect of employees. Achievement of forward work plan. Reduction of functional and departmental costs. Increase in functional and departmental return and/or volume. Reduction of 'noise' around points of lower performance (inefficiency, low profit, money wastage, low engagement, poor customer service).	Miss and/or expose holes in the strategic plan. Fail to deliver strategic outcomes. Executive censure. Public censure. Reputational risk (personal and organisational). Ridicule of colleagues and staff. Being fired or demoted.

Stakeholder type	Do want from the change	Don't want from the change
Regulators	More compliance.	Less compliance.
	Safer.	More hazardous.
	More standardised.	Less standardised.
	More efficient.	Less efficient.
	Enhanced reputation for the regulation.	Criticism of the regulator's role and credibility.
	Respect of colleagues and peers, fellow regulatory organisations.	

The table doesn't say, 'want to make a positive contribution to the lives of the change recipients'. I would dearly like to write this in as a given. In a perfect world it would be. But in my experience, 'it ain't necessarily so'. There are more basic motivators. These boil down to 'seek gain, avoid pain'. Making the lives of the change recipients better is often a secondary motivation. A by-product of the gain. It is a step that gets you to 'seek gain, avoid pain'. It would be great to write in for the change initiator, 'A servant leader who genuinely wants to help the change recipients'. This is the 'lucky country' for a change manager or anyone else tasked with delivering business change. But in a thirty-year career, I've experienced this only on three projects. It is a particular brand of sun we all crave and, boy, what a difference it makes! But don't count on it. Really, I've got to a stage where I've realised there's no shame in being driven by more personal motivators like 'look good to colleagues' if those motivate you to model traits of the servant leader. Perhaps this is more honestly how it really works.

Remember chapter 1. If you're clear on how the change aligns to your values, you know why you're there. Then you can work with a wide range of the motivations in this table. A lot of them aren't 'bad';

they just don't have quite the selflessness of the semi-mythical servant leader, at least, not in the first instance. If you do work with a real, bona fide, 'live in the wild' servant leader, then big congrats. You caught a unicorn.

Group 2—Change partners—what they want and don't want

Stakeholder type	Want from the change	Don't want from the change
Subject matter experts	To be listened to. To be seen as an expert. Positive reference. More work. Work satisfaction (feel that they add value).	To be ignored. To be undermined. Humiliated in front of peers, manager, colleagues. Reputational damage.
Vendors	The next sale. A positive reference site. To maximise the profit made from the contract. To meet the time and materials agreements made in the contract. Secure the ongoing maintenance contract. Get an 'in' to secure more work from the client.	To lose money. Bad client reference. Scope creep. Reputational damage.

	Close alignment to what was requested and what they understood, 'no surprises'. To do interesting work, innovate whilst 'on the clock'.	
Media	Juicy stories—unfolding drama. Political hot buttons pushed. Human interest angles. Spectacular success or failure. Wrongs righted or wrongs revealed.	Event-free delivery with no drama. Lack of commentary and/or visibility of issues at play. Lack of clarity on outcomes.
Lobby groups	Key lobby agenda progressed or achieved. Lobby issues get more visibility. Core wrong righted. Perceived justice. Improved rights for their supporters. Increased group membership. Increased profile for group.	Negative publicity and/or ridicule of cause. Counter issue given increased attention. Discreditation. Loss of membership.
Unions	Increased rights and entitlements for members.	Decrease in rights and/or entitlements for members.

	Opportunities for members.	Reduced opportunity for members.
	Increase in membership and subscriptions.	Decrease in membership and subscriptions.
	Increase in respect for union and delegates.	Loss of credibility and/or respect for the union.
	Increased opportunities to air issues.	Loss of credibility and/or respect for the union delegate.
	Improved access to senior leaders.	Lost jobs for members.
	Positive media coverage.	Decrease in union reach and power.

Group 3—Change recipients—what they want and don't want

Now we get to the change recipients. Ideally, this group takes precedence. You know you've got your work cut out for you when the project treats this group like an afterthought. Yes, this happens. Worse is when the change initiators group think users' motivations are the same as theirs.

Stakeholder type	Want from the change	Don't want from the change
Users	Quicker. Easier. More efficient. More value. More recognition.	Slower. More steps. Harder. Reduced access. Less effective.

	More opportunity. More interesting. More status. More money. More personalised. More features. More convenient. More accessible. More skills.	Less personal. Less accessible. More boring. Less status. Job loss.
Consumers	More for less. More range. More features. Increased quality. Increased efficiency. Less expensive. More availability. Easier. More authentic.	Less for the same. Less for more. Reduced options. Reduced support. Fewer features. Substitutions—inferior product. Harder. Less accessible. Less authentic.
Clients	More personal. More features. More fun. More value. More customised More convenient. Easier. More accessible. More authentic. More status.	Less personal. Fewer features. Less convenient. Less accessible. Less value. Less quality. Harder. Less convenient. Less authentic. Less status.

Finally, last, but not least, there are the interested onlookers. This group can be easy to miss. But don't underestimate them. Their ability to influence for change adoption or block it is significant.

Group 4—Interested onlookers—what they want and don't want

Stakeholder type	Want from the change	Don't want from the change
Interested onlookers	Makes their job easier or the same. Streamlines relationships. Cuts down steps in process. Streamlines operational model. Reduces requirement to intervene. Increases their power and status and/or that of their group and/or function.	Make their job harder. Gives their boss more headaches. Makes things more complicated. Increases steps in process Increases requirement to intervene. Moves power and/or status somewhere else.

How to use the tables above

The tables above are a distillation of my experience of what the most common incentives and disincentives are for each stakeholder group in any change. If I had ten bucks for every time I've used something in these tables to motivate stakeholder change adoption, I'd have a fat stack of cash.

You can use these tables as a primer. They will help you understand what any stakeholder group in a change process really wants and doesn't want.

Now that we have a high-level sense of these key stakeholders, let's look at how to capture them in your stakeholder assessment.

What to capture in a stakeholder assessment

A stakeholder assessment is a table that captures all your stakeholders. It then identifies their interest in and attitude to the upcoming change.

There are hundreds of variants on the format of a stakeholder assessment. I've worked with a lot of them. When it comes to templates, there's no 'perfect' template. There is only the perfect template customised to YOUR change initiative and how you like to work. In my experience the stakeholder assessment is most useful in the first third of the project. Then it's useful again just prior and during delivery. In the design and development phases you should be too busy to put a lot of energy into maintaining these. If you are spending a lot of time on this throughout your project, it's counterproductive. These documents are a snapshot, at a fixed point in time. Much of what they cover is quite subjective. You want to be clear with your senior stakeholders on this when you set them up before they're taken as gospel.

Maintenance of these documents really shouldn't suck up enormous time and energy. That's not good. Spend more time with your stakeholders than with your documents (*about* your stakeholders). You can see the irony there if it's the wrong way round. At the start of a project a decent stakeholder assessment is crucial. It helps you to understand the stakeholder landscape. This means you can confidently describe it back to your stakeholder groups. You need to map it out. Then you can play it back to make sure everyone's views align. You are sense-making and then validating that sense-making. This is a key function of the change manager role. You're also providing assurance to these key stakeholders that the change manager knows what they're doing. A stakeholder assessment is one of the first major deliverables you produce on a project.

The stakeholder assessment is never complete. Yet, it is an essential playback tool of the change manager. Use it to show you have a grasp on who's playing, what they want, and how you'll enable them.

There are so many columns you CAN have in a stakeholder assessment. But a lot of time can be wasted on highly subjective content.

This is things like, 'what they want from the change', and 'best communication medium'. The first one might change week to week and the second one is often a default. In most organisations the key channels and mediums for communications are already determined. Examples would be the monthly departmental newsletter, or the people leaders weekly email update. I wouldn't use too many categories like these. Just do an initial population to get general agreement when the landscape is mapped out. Then spend a little bit of maintenance time on it maybe every couple of weeks. The main thing is to add new stakeholders as you find them. The work here is never done. New stakeholders always pop out of the woodwork. The capture of these emerging stakeholders IS crucial. You must capture them so that their needs are known and accommodated. Then they won't derail your go-live.

The document becomes key again close to delivery. That's about three to four months out from the go-live target. Use it to get to the point where you have current email addresses and other specifics like role and location for your change recipients. For external change recipients, mobile numbers and addresses may also be crucial depending on what you're delivering.

Stakeholder assessment template

Here's my template for a usable stakeholder assessment, one that's realistic to maintain.

Name	Role	Email	Location	Impact	Current perception of change	What they want	Primary engagement method
				High (red). Med (amber). Low (green).			

You often see other categories like 'desired perception of the change' included. But it's a given that you want them to be in favour of the change, right? (Or at the least, neutral). So why bother writing that in endless rows?

How to capture your stakeholders

Once you start on a business change initiative, it's time to start the stakeholder assessment. In the first couple of days you're on the team, you'll hear about 60 percent of the core stakeholders. You should be noting them down. Use your preferred method of capture such as OneNote, Word, Excel. If you're like me, kick it old school with a paper notebook. Often what you hear on the first couple of days will form the basis of all your key change deliverables. That's if you have a decent project manager, sponsor, and some 'on to it' subject matter experts (SMEs) who can brief you.

The next step is to widen the input by getting stakeholders together. Workshop 'outwards' from your core stakeholders. The more people you talk to, the more people you need to talk to. It's a positive sign when people stop referring you to other people. In each meeting ask, 'Is there anyone else you think I should talk to? Why?' That's how you find all the concentric rings of engagement you need to cover.

If you don't have time or resources to run extensive workshops, use a straw model. Bring something to the table to get traction. Building by 'pushing off' something is always quicker than starting with a blank piece of paper. Have you ever noticed how meetings with no input to focus on tend to meander? Of course, it depends on the size of the business change and the constraints on getting access to stakeholders. If the project's on the medium to large side, I'd recommend running a decent stakeholder workshop. This works better as a series of workshops if you have more than around eight key groups. It's amazing what you can learn when you get all these stakeholders together. There will be plenty of dynamics to observe! Be attuned to them. You can learn a lot from these sessions on where your road-blocks will be. Sometimes more than you wanted to! Particularly if relationships between key teams in the change are particularly acrimonious. This happens a fair bit. This is also your first inkling of what will make the change stick. That's a feeling sense of how this group dynamic will respond to the proposed change.

Common dynamics between stakeholder groups

Here's a primer on some of the key dynamics you might notice in these workshops.

- One of the upstream processing teams has a grudge with a downstream team. They feel the other team gets all the attention, resources, and kudos.

- The policy team feels that the operational team who implements their policy doesn't 'get it'. They don't work hard enough or smart enough to make the policy work. They 'cut corners'.

- The operational team thinks the policy team lives in an 'ivory tower'. They think policy has no real idea of how things work in the 'real world'. That means the developed policy isn't practical.

- The risk team feels the operational team doesn't pay enough attention to the risks.

- The operational team feels the risk team never focuses enough on opportunities.

- The regulator thinks the operational team doesn't follow the regulatory policy closely enough.

- The operational team thinks the regulatory team cares more about rules than delivery.

- The team doesn't like the boss.

- The staff doesn't like or respect the chief executive or the executive team.

- The staff feels the executives are too scared to make decisions.

- The staff thinks the executives never do the hard prioritisation. That means too much is done badly, rather than 'a few things done well'.

- The chief executive (CE) and/or the executive team think the staff like and respect them, but they're wrong.

- The staff thinks leaders see them as a high-performing team, but they're wrong.

- The executives are too busy jostling for position with the CE and against each other. They have no time or attention for the real business change, or the needs of their people.

- The staff feels the executive is completely disconnected from the real business environment. It's 'them' and 'us'.

- The operational team thinks the strategy or customer experience or marketing or sales team is the 'favourite child'. They have the flashiest office space on the best floor in the best building. They get the highest wages and have senior leader access whenever they want it.

- The executives think they have too many legacy 'low-performing' employees. But also few performance management options to change it. It would also be a media sh!t storm to performance manage out the underperformers, so it's not done. The reputational risk is too great. Maybe even career limiting.

- The operational teams think the support functions aren't responsive. They create too many barriers.

- The support functions think that the operations teams undervalue their contribution.

- The generalists think there are too many experts with 'narrow but deep' expertise. They don't see the end-to-end picture.
- The experts think the generalists look 'too broadly but not deeply'. They feel the generalists don't understand the complex issues. That means they don't make informed decisions on the hard stuff.

That's a fair representation of the most common dynamics I see among teams and individuals. If you are aware of these tensions, you can use them to inform the view of where the hardest points will be to make the change stick. Watch for these dynamics, capture them early, and begin formulating your mitigations. A lot of them will require you to exercise the art of the constructive compromise.

Tips on how to run stakeholder assessment workshops

If you get the luxury of running a face-to-face workshop, then doing a sticky notes exercise off a few key structured questions can be fruitful. The kind of questions you want to ask are these eight.

1. Who will be impacted by this business change?
2. Who else will be affected by it?
3. Who else wants to know about the change and why?
4. Who are the main players internally?
5. Who are the main players externally?
6. Who would it be easy to forget and why?
7. How will each group feel about the business change and why?
8. What would change that feeling?

Microsoft Teams is pretty standard for running virtual workshops these days. You can support sessions with Microsoft Whiteboard or other collaboration tools like Miro. Or you can give each participant a workbook. This is electronic, but the participant can print it if they prefer. Gather these in at the end or, even better, capture the output on a virtual Lean Canvas, a one-page business plan template. Miro is great for this and pretty easy to use.

The stakeholder assessment is one of the first maps to help understand 'the edges of scope'. *Scope,* when it comes to stakeholders, is usually soft focus and opaque. It's hard to see those edges, and they can shift. You are at the start of sense-making when the stakeholder assessment begins to emerge.

If it's a big piece of business change, it works well to take an end-to-end process approach in workshops. Use the process sequence to map out the stakeholders and the impacts on each group. The process stages give you key road map junctions on which to 'hang' the impacts. Start your workshop with the first thing that happens in the business change. Look at all the stakeholders related to that stage. Then look at each stage ongoing until you get to the end and the process loops back to the beginning.

Example of how to understand the change through the process life-cycle

Here's an example. Let's say the business change is in banking and relates to a new credit card product.

You can understand these stakeholders through the credit card product life cycle. This starts with all the product creation and sales areas. This is followed by marketing, card procurement, distribution, operational administration and revenue gathering, complaint resolution, and card decommissioning.

Note that stakeholder assessments are like archaeological digs. The more you dig, the more you unearth. It's important to keep digging.

Remember that as a change enabler, you must check what you hear. Teams will perceive the same information in different ways. Ask the same question at least three times of different people before you're satisfied the answer is legit. If three different people say approximately the same thing, then it's probably as right as it can be for now. Keep performing the validation process throughout the project.

Summary

That's the end of chapter 2. Now you understand how to divide your key stakeholders up into groups according to their relationship to the change. It also provides a high-level walk-through of how to gather your stakeholder assessment and the key questions to ask to map it out. The four key stakeholder groups in any change are these.

1. The change initiators 'above' the change.
2. The change partners 'on' the change.
3. The change recipients 'in' the change (journey).
4. The interested onlookers 'around' the change.

To qualify your stakeholder assessment you must identify each group in these four categories. Then ask the following two questions for each group.

1. What do they want in relation to the change?
2. What are the things they don't want from the change?

The core message of this chapter is that all stakeholders are human beings. They want to move toward gain and away from pain. You must understand each stakeholder type first. How do they relate to the change? Then understand what the move toward gain and away from pain looks like to them. A stakeholder assessment is always 'in action'. You don't finish it. Rather, you flow with it in a constant unfolding.

In the next chapter, we'll look at how to get to the heart of the change. This chapter covers how to identify the change impacts. These are the impacts that truly matter to each group to make it stick. That's what gives them permission to make the change.

CHAPTER 3

Find the Truth of the Change

T eams receive a lot of business change where they have no clue what the value is TO THEM. This is a true 'sad face' moment for any change manager who cares about high adoption. This book isn't about the appalling statistics about how many change initiatives fail.[4] But generally, change projects fail because they didn't get this step right. The unique value to each key stakeholder group wasn't correctly identified and sold to the right audience.

What's delivered that truly matters to each impacted group?

In 2020, I joined a sizeable project in the public sector. When I joined up, the project was only a couple of weeks out from go-live. It was a very hierarchical organisation. The project to date had told the senior stakeholders what it thought they wanted to hear. Change recipients had heard, well, almost nothing. At least, nothing specific about how the change affected their day-to-day work.

This is a double whammy. It's quite a common combination to join a project and find the change initiators were told the wrong thing and the change recipients were told nothing. This usually reflects that at the start of the project the stakeholder assessment wasn't as complete or accurate as required. This is why it's so important to be clear about what EACH of your key stakeholder groups wants from the change. Then give these messages the airtime they need to the right audience.

There's often real tension between what change initiators and change recipients value. You are there to broker the change to these groups in a way that gives each the outcome that motivates them. You can't sell to the change recipients what the change initiators want. These different populations have completely different needs and drivers. Of course, the change initiators, who are usually the bosses, set the initial agenda. But the outcomes they value must be reframed in a way that has genuine appeal and pulling power for the other stakeholder audiences. It is part of the role of the change manager to explain this requirement to the change initiators. It's almost a sleight of hand to help leaders understand that if they want their outcomes, they have to permit others to extract their own distinct outcomes. When change projects do fail, you can usually trace it back to a confusion of who values what and the wrong audience being sold the wrong thing.

Let's look further at the project I mention above. This project delivered a new approach to funding bid development and submission for local councils seeking government funding to complete public works.

Here are the contrasting outcomes statements used on this project to reset the stakeholders' expectations.

Change Initiators Value Proposition	Change Recipients Value Proposition
Collective, cumulative enterprise value	**Individual and team value**
More transparent, traceable, standardised, and repeatable process. This will lead to more cost-effective, equitable, and future-proofed funding decisions.	The change brings ease through faster, easier, more supported, and more effective funding bids.
We fund the right things, in the right way at the right time.	It's easier to write and submit a funding bid.
The public works programme has a more cost-effective funding return and higher cumulative benefit realisation that closely align to our strategic goals.	It's easier to match local projects to the funding criteria.
	There's a better chance of submitting an effective bid. This means faster funding bid submission, less rework, and an increased chance of approval.
	The public works funded are more sustainable, effective, and future-proofed.

Staff and executive leaders usually want completely different things. They operate in a different context. They need different things on the change horizon to motivate. There's also a significant power imbalance between them. It's easy for the leaders to assume that everyone else wants what they want. But it's not easy for employees to call out that they don't want what the leaders tell them they want! That's until a couple of months before go-live. Then all hell will break loose (as it did on the project I mention above). When this disconnect in what's valued surfaces before go-live, employees really don't care about what the leaders want. They'll demand to know what they do, step by step on day one and how they'll get support to do it.

It's just before go-live. For the moment, you've bypassed your change recipients caring about the outcomes. At this point, it's all about the WHAT and HOW and little about the why. People just want to know in detail WHAT THEY DO once the flag drops. That's the bottom line on how this plays out. This shift happens about three or four months out from go-live. Be prepped with the meaningful and emotionally resonant outcome statements well before this.

On the project I mention above, I revamped the stakeholder assessment. Then I worked through the stakeholder list to reset their understanding and commitment. First off were the general managers. Those who led internal change recipients. After the revamped briefing, one general manager reached out to my boss's boss. They told them that finally someone had explained to them what the project was about. Now they understood what it would deliver and how it affected their teams. At that time, the project had been running for two years (and was two weeks out from delivery). You might think that's weird and unusual, but actually it's weird and not unusual!

I share this to illustrate how important it is to get the basics right. Chapters 1, 2, and 3 cover these basics. They are your blueprint to define the change in a way that is meaningful to each group.

This is like a Rubik's Cube, as I said before. What each stakeholder group cares about depends on what face they have 'turned toward the change'. For a vendor, it might be a business opportunity. For interested onlookers, it's a new philosophy on how to operate. For the operational teams, it's a demanding re-think of what they do, step-by-step in each working day, whereas for the CE, it might be a last-ditch effort to get the 'runs on the board' that got them the job.

You have to identify the right value statement for each group. Otherwise, their eyes will 'bounce off the change'.

Common ways the value proposition gets confused

Here is a list of the other common ways that the value proposition for the change gets confused.

Example 1: The project describes the value as widgets rather than outcomes. 'The project will deliver a funding bid approach. There are tools and templates for how to use the approach. You get access to a new information management portal.'

This is missing what the outcomes and benefits of the deliverables will be. Also, why the change recipients should care emotionally.

Example 2: The project describes the value as outputs and not outcomes. 'The project will deliver a new system application. The application will automatically make credit scoring decisions.'

This is a variant on example 1 above. It is missing what the outcomes and benefits of the deliverables will be. And again, also why the change recipients should care.

Example 3: The project describes the value as features and not benefits. 'The project will deliver a portal that will be available twenty-four-seven.'

This is better—but it still does not spell it out. What's the benefits of a portal available twenty-four-seven? This should tell a story about ease of use and convenience.

Example 4: The project does manage to describe itself in outcomes. But without any emotional appeal. 'You'll get a quicker, more accurate, and more consistent credit decision.'

Still not there. This needs to sell the sizzle. Add on, 'So that you can plan your future with more certainty.' Is the dream about travelling? A new home or renovation? Starting a family? A new hobby?

To get change adoption and make it stick, you have to bring the value to life. Communicate the change as if the outcome the stakeholder values were here now. Place the stakeholder in the future state, experiencing the value that motivates. Do it so they experience an emotional connection to that value. You want to speak to the heart of the value the change adoption brings. Make it specific and make it personal. This is what makes it stick. Speak to them and them only. Say it in easy, conversational ways. In the language of 'lived experience'. Draw the change recipient into the emotional charge. They must picture themselves as successful, enriched in the future state.

Don't focus on the 'things' delivered. Think about the value delivered and the emotional charge associated with it. Find a way to describe the positive emotions people will experience if they adopt the change.

The formula looks like this:

**Key outcomes stakeholder receives + Emotional charge
of the value received = Permission to change**

Ineffective and effective outcome statements

Example table of ineffective and effective outcome statements.

	Don't do this	Do this	to get this compelling emotional response
Stakeholder Audience	**Widget or feature or output change impact statement**	**Outcome- or feature-based impact statement**	**Emotional charge**
Local Council Funding Applicants	• A new funding bid approach. • Tools and templates. • A new information management repository about investment funding. • New benefits realisation measures.	A simplified funding bid approach. It's quick and easy to see what's likely to be funded. There'll be no more time wasted submitting ineligible business cases for things that don't meet criteria. You'll get tools and templates that fill in key fields for you and do the heavy lifting with calculations. It's easier and less time-consuming	**Excited** to anticipate a new and more exciting work experience. **Happy** to have a more supported work experience. **Relieved** to have less menial, difficult, and time-consuming work. **Relieved** to have less chance of their funding bid being declined.

		to develop your financials. Step-by-step guidance makes development and submission faster and less painful. There are new benefits realisation measures so there are no benefit types that don't fit and can't be assessed. This means better, more sustainable, and future-proofed investment decision-making.	**Motivated** to embrace the opportunity to do more successful and valued work.
Banking customers with a mortgage (existing and new)	The project will deliver a new revolving credit home loan product.	This new revolving credit account helps you make your money work harder. Every time your salary or other earnings are paid into your revolving credit account, you'll reduce the interest payments on your mortgage.	**Happy** to reduce interest on home loan. **Excited** to reduce term of home loan. **Relieved** to simplify account structure. **Happy** to have a way to manage fluctuating cash flow more effectively.

		This means your money works harder for you, and it is managed out of one single account.	
Front Line Lenders	The project will deliver a new system application. This will automatically make the less complex credit scoring decisions.	You won't have to touch the simple lending applications if all eligibility criteria are met. You'll be freed up to make the more complex and high value lending decisions. You can win more high value complex business and help more people achieve their dreams. You're doing work that counts in a thriving organisation that contributes to a prosperous country.	**Happy** to be relieved of menial, repetitious box-checking work. **Excited** about opportunities to do more interesting work. **Eager** to win more high value business and be seen to win that business. **Proud** to do what matters and contributes to society.

A big part of your work will be allaying initial fears that any automation work isn't about shedding staff. That is if it's really not about that. If it is about that, see chapter 1 to check the values alignment.

The bottom line is that none of your stakeholders cares about widgets. They care about the value the widgets can deliver to them, to make their working day easier, more varied, more satisfying, more productive, and more valued.

Notice how the final column in the table above is all about the movement toward gain and away from pain. For example, 'happy', 'excited' (moving toward pleasure), 'relieved' (avoiding pain). At its heart, human psychology is about these simple things. People are infinitely complex, but these motivators are not. They're very simple and universal.

People will move toward your change if it delivers value. You must tell a story that gives them the experience of feeling that value. Picture them successful in the future state. Give them an experience of the opportunity. Lay the bread crumb trail.

A final note on widgets. When you're doing projects or business as usual (BAU) initiatives. things get busy, really busy. When you're busy, the pressure is on. There's always a danger the project can become a cottage industry. A self-sustaining organism. One that believes its own hype and marks its own report card. In my funding bid approach example, you may ask, How did it get so off course? How did outcome and value get so lost? What happened was that the impact statements were developed very early on. Things weren't clear, as the project was 'working things out as it went along'. Deliverables changed over the two years between conception and delivery. There were strong drivers to give the senior leaders good news. That 'good news' became the default. This is not uncommon.

The bigger they are, the more this happens. Things can get enshrined as incontrovertible facts on big projects very fast. Quicker than you can say 'low hanging fruit' or 'cadence' (winky face). Big projects can involve hundreds of internal and consulting employees. They have complex governance and hierarchical structures. That's a lot of pressure not to 'subvert the dominant paradigm' right there. The peer pressure to 'toe the party line' within the project tribe can be immense. Times it by warp factor five if you have a sponsor who doesn't like bad news.

This all depends, of course, on the culture of the project. The tone of which is set by the sponsor and the project and/or programme manager. Change leaders, change managers, and change agents must stay focussed on the objective. There is a duty of care implicit in the role to keep the project honest. To call out anything that smacks of 'the emperor's new clothes'. It's much easier to make small course corrections throughout, than to make a massive upheaval at the end, as happened on the new funding bid example above. To increase the odds of high adoption, course correct often and with determination. Get to the heart of why people would want to experience the change and what that would feel like for them when they do. Frequently, there will be negotiation with change initiators to help them understand the different stakeholder perspectives and accept that the value looks different on each side of the Rubik's Cube.

Projects gather their own rhetoric faster than a snowball gathers snow as it speeds downhill. The project rhetoric can help or hinder. 'Look at all our lovely widgets' is a crap message. This is not the high ground. And at the point of change delivery, the force will not be with you. It's not enough to get the project delivered; you want to get it adopted and make the change stick. This only happens if people feel the life of the change. The dynamic value that they will personally realise if they move into it. Change managers are the conscience of the project. You must give the project the heart that enables the change. That means statements of specific and meaningful value targeted to each stakeholder.

Change Cat knew... change
is about Permission NOT
control!

Permission NOT CONTROL

Using the outcomes onion to get to the heart of the change

The outcomes onion is a tool I've used for years. Use it to get to the heart of the change for each key stakeholder group. This exercise helps ensure we're talking about outcomes with an emotional pull. Outcomes described in ways that are meaningful and resonant to the stakeholder. We're not talking about widgets, features, or outputs here. Focus on outcomes—the pleasure or gain the change moves us toward and the pain it helps us avoid.

Outcomes onion exercise

The exercise is simple. Draw yourself a picture of a half onion showing some concentric rings (no prizes for art skills here!). On the outer circle of your onion, write in what your main stakeholder group gets when the change lands. Now ask, 'And so what about that?' Keep on writing statements and asking, 'And so what?' When you can't write another statement 'inside' the last, you've got to the heart of the change.

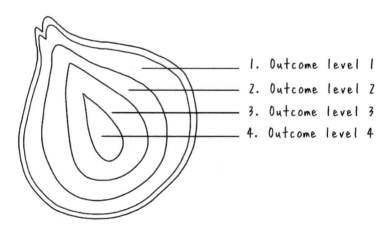

Outcomes Onion

1. Outcome level 1
2. Outcome level 2
3. Outcome level 3
4. Outcome level 4

Worked example: New business funding approach outcome onion

For the new funding bid approach project discussed above, the outer circle of the onion looked like this.

1. Local councils get a new funding bid approach. There are tools and templates for business case development. There's also access to an information repository about funding investment.

   Now ask yourself, 'And so what about that? What's good about it? Why would people care? What are they getting out of it that motivates them to use that?'

2. You, the local councils, will have more direction on what types of projects are eligible for funding. This saves time and effort in your business case development and submission process.

   Again, 'So what about that?'

3. It's easier and more efficient to develop and submit a business case. You'll get more direction on what's required and how to structure it. There are automated macros to help you complete the financials.

   And 'So what about that?'

4. You have a great chance of submitting a quality funding bid that meets the eligibility criteria. This helps get a successful business case funded quicker.

Ah! Now we're getting to it! What do local councils want when they submit funding bids? They want approved funding in a quick turn-around time. They DON'T want funding bid re-work, resubmission, and declines.

Toward gain and away from pain

In chapter 2 we first introduced the idea of stakeholder movement toward gain and away from pain. Note this doesn't preclude accepting some pain for greater pleasure and/or gain at a later date. But delayed gratification can only happen if the amygdala stays calm. That only happens if the prefrontal cortex saddles up the amygdala (emotional trigger centre) and rides it back to the corral. When we socialise a change, we must speak to the heart of the outcome onion. How you first position a business change really matters. Otherwise, the amygdala will be activated at the first hint of change. No point trying to deliver quality rational messages when the amygdala is shouting, 'Fire! Fire!' You have to soothe the fear response before you can deliver positive value messages.

Worked funding bid approach example

Here is a summary of impact statements that move toward gain and away from pain.

Change recipients move toward	Change recipients move away from
Successful approval of business case funding bid.	Extra work re-drafting and submitting rejected business cases.
Faster approval timeframe.	Longer timeframes to decision.
Respect of boss and peers for successful submission.	Decline of funding approval.

Let's talk about the work you may need to do with your sponsor, steering group, and even project manager to get this right. Sometimes internal business people are seconded into these senior roles. They may have had no previous experience delivering business change projects. Here's the internal dialogue from senior leaders that leads to this. 'This is a business project built off what the policy team developed. Linda has been a senior manager in policy for many years. They really understand policy. That means she would make a great sponsor or business owner or product manager.'

This is a challenge. This person could actually be the WORST person to lead the change. Linda is a policy wonk. That means she carries a lot of unconscious assumptions that everyone else is a policy wonk. She knows the subject matter too well. Also, she is possibly more concerned with the form than the intent of the policy. Is she a policy purist, or is she a pragmatist? Does she understand how to design policy that actually works in the real world? If she has been a senior policy manager for a long time, chances are she may be quite disconnected from what works at the coalface. Even oblivious if she has always worked in policy and never seen how it works on the ground. If she also lacks understanding of the change journey, it's a double whammy. Her unconscious assumptions may mean she thinks everyone will immediately leap to adoption.

Once we've made it, we all tend to forget our own adoption journey. Can you remember how long it took you to learn to drive a car? Or the challenges you had to overcome to become so proficient that you don't have to consciously think about how to drive anymore to do it? Once unconscious competence is reached, it's very easy to underestimate how long the journey will take for others.

I summarise this as the 'field of dreams' syndrome. These types of change initiators think 'If you build it, they (the change recipients) will come.' Believe me, they won't. I hope the last two chapters make it clear why this is untrue. If you build it, they won't come. That's unless you give them a compelling reason to WANT to. That only happens if you sell things in a way that has a personal and compelling emotional resonance. Change initiators often have a lot of unconscious assumptions. They forget what doesn't translate to others. The change manager must coach an awareness of the gap. Then they must draw the line to outcomes that will bridge that gap.

Summary

That's the end of chapter 3. This chapter teaches you how to craft meaningful outcome statements. That's a statement with a compelling emotional resonance. Statements that make people WANT to adopt the change. You've learned to think beyond widgets. To think of the deep truth of the change. These are statements that speak to each stakeholder group, from THEIR perspective. The beating heart of the change. This is what motivates and makes change stick. This is what draws people in. This makes your change an opportunity to move toward gain and away from pain.

The core message of this chapter is that your stakeholders doesn't care about widgets. They care about outcomes that move them toward gain and away from pain. Identify for each group the pleasure and/

or reward the change will bring. Then, what is the pain the change will help them avoid? Craft a compelling story related to these movements, a story about the feeling experience of the pleasure gained and the pain avoided. Make sure not to confuse what the change initiators want with what the change recipients want.

In the next chapter, we'll look at how to hone your outcomes into effective 'What's in it for me' statements (WIIFMs). To do that, we first have to understand how to create an effective change impact assessment.

CHAPTER 4

The Change Impact Assessment and 'What's in it for Me?'

Now we're ready to talk about the change impact assessment. The change impact assessment is the 'one ring to rule them all' for successful change delivery. At the centre of the impact assessment are quality 'what's in it for me' (WIIFM) statements. These must be acutely stakeholder specific.

WIIFMs that work and WIIFMs that don't

Change impact assessments are usually in table format, in Word or Excel. These documents identify each key item that will change in the future state. They define the gap between the current state and the future state. The future state is after the business change implements. A good change impact assessment is an insurance policy for 'no ugly surprises' at go-live. The change impact assessment is the intentional anticipation of unintended consequences.

The WIIFM falls out of the change gap statement in your impact assessment. Gap statements must describe what is different between 'now' and 'then', after the change happens. The statements need to be as clear and explicit as possible. They must nail why the change recipient should care about the difference between now and then. The WIIFM is your sell for why the change user would want to successfully make the journey from here to there. The WIIFM articulates the value of the journey.

Overall, the purpose of the change impact assessment is these five things.

1. Provide a single source of truth for all the changes that are happening.

2. Capture specifics on who's impacted and in what ways. Then it explains the support to the impacted people to go through the change.

3. Capture the WIIFM. This provides the compelling, point-specific reasons why anyone would change.

4. Sell the emotional charge of the change adoption to make it stick.

5. Provide traceability between the development of business requirements and use cases and how these have been interpreted into impacts by the change team.

You can access an endless amount of information about change impact assessments. There are also myriads of opinions about what should be in one, and how to 'slice and dice' the information.

To cut to the chase, below is my preferred template for a change impact assessment. This is in the order in which items are best captured. The bit that matters most is the gap statement, the WIIFMs column. This 'sells the sizzle'. Sometimes I've seen change impact assessments that have no gap statements. That's a big mistake. You just lost the heart of the document. If you don't include the gap statements, you are 100 percent more likely to miss the heart of the change, so your chances of adoption just nosedived.

Here are the key summary points of what an ineffective WIIFM focuses on.

1. Ineffective WIIFMs tend to be corporate speak and/or technical jargon. They express the change from the perspective of what 'management' wants. That's the change initiator group. They don't speak to what the change recipient wants.

2. Ineffective WIIFMs don't highlight what the movement toward gain and away from pain is.

3. Ineffective WIIFMs focus on widgets, not outcomes.

4. Ineffective WIIFMs lack 'colour' or emotional charge. They don't 'sell the sizzle' or address the barriers to adoption.

5. Ineffective WIIFMs use clinical language. They focus on facts and don't appeal to the emotional side of our nature. (Emotions often trump logic, right?)

6. Ineffective WIIFMs claim high ground they're not entitled to. They lack authenticity.

7. Ineffective WIIFMs assume that change initiators, change partners, and change recipients want the same thing. Usually they don't. Not really. Even if they might tell you they do. Watch out for that passive agreement at the start of your change engagement. It means the culture sucks, and it's 'not safe' to say what you really think and feel. Then you need to take a stealth approach and learn the culture. Then work out how to positively influence it through safe one-on-one sessions with your best stakeholders. Those are the ones who will share with you what's really going on and what change recipients really think and feel.

WIIFMs for 'Project Cat Foods'—projects that are about negative consequence

Here are some special notes for compliance change projects and others that are about the avoidance of negative consequence. I call these 'project cat food' types. This is a nickname for projects that aren't delivering anything sexy or desirable. Usually, they are regulatory compliance changes. Sometimes they're operational tidy-up or general housekeeping pieces. These types of projects are usually imposed on an organisation by an external party. Usually, it's regulators or new government legislation. It's a 'project cat food' because no one wants it in the fridge. It has to be there, but nobody wants it (except Change Cat of course!).

There are plenty of them about and there's no shame in working on them. Often, they're easier in some ways if they're mandatory. But a special note on gap statements and WIIFMs for these. Don't try to blag it. That means—don't try and make out it's fabulous, and a big win when it's not. If the project is about avoiding negative consequence, then be upfront about that. If there's significant financial or social or reputational penalty if it's not done, then say so. Definitely don't try and make out like 'we wanted it all along'. That is a classic 'I smell a rat' move. The deception will always be found out. Not even found out, maybe just known. Intuited by culture as soon as you try to pull a swifty. This is the type of duplicity that culture has a restless hypervigilance for.

I once worked on a real 'project cat food' known as the 'Foreign Account Tax Compliance Act', or FATCA for short. This required banks to report their US-born clients to the local tax authority. The requirement was mandated via government legislation. The local tax authority would collect information from the banks and

Project

report on eligible customers to the Inland Revenue Service (IRS) in the United States.

When I first started on the project, a general manager asked me, 'How are you going to sell the change?' I replied, I wasn't, as no one wants to buy a 'cup of cold sick'. It got me a look, for sure. But I painted a clear picture with the GM that we would not be attempting to lipstick the pig. That it would be foolish to try. These projects need different tactics. We had to make a compelling case for how the negative consequence of not complying was so great, non-compliance was not an option. We also had to play the 'poor me' card. As in, 'we're not the bad guy here'. The story was 'we really don't want to do it', but the 'mean old' government and/or banking association is making us. Waaaaah!

Change initiators, that is usually the general managers, directors, and executives, are always looking for good news. They have to be cheerleaders 'shakin' hands and kissin' babies' on a regular rotation. If you're the change manager on a 'project cat food', you have to keep these change initiators honest. It's much more authentic to own the truth that a negative consequence drives these changes rather than to try to sell it as a fist-pump moment. Bottom line—don't pretend it's sexy when it ain't.

A few months into 'Project FATCA', I presented to the digital team. In question time, someone asked why the project had such a 'dumb' name. The answer, of course, was that 'it does what it says on the tin'. It would be disingenuous to call these 'Project Snowball' or 'Project Phoenix'. The use of jazzy graphics and rocket ship icons would be worse. That's committing a multitude of sins.

If it's a dog, then say it's a dog (gently). But be clear about the dog's bite if it's not complied with.

Research shows that the avoidance of pain is a compelling motivator anyway.[5] Your burning case for change is a doddle on these! In the case of FATCA, there were multi-billion-dollar penalties if it wasn't complied with.

The gap statement WIIFMs for FATCA looked like this

Current State	Future State	Gap Statement	Gap Statement WIIFMs
No requirement to report US-born financial services customers to the IRS.	All US-born customers must be reported to US taxation services. Their IRS numbers must also be provided if known.	From 1 July 2014 we're obligated to report customers who were born in the US to the Inland Revenue Service (IRS).	As of 1 July 2014, the FATCA legislation passed into New Zealand law. From this date we are required to report our customers who were born in the US to the taxation agency which would then report it to the IRS. All major banks in the country are obligated to comply. If we fail to comply, we're in breach of legislation. The Banking Association of New Zealand has put out a pamphlet to explain to all banking customers what FATCA is and why the banking industry must comply. We've used data analytics to determine our likely reportable customers. We'll be sending prepared letters to all likely affected customers. This will prepare them for 1 July and explain to them what their likely obligations are and how to fulfil them.

In the last column above, let's break down what's been made clear to the customer and the underlying message. That's the emotional appeal to the customer, shown here in italics.

1. What the change is. A compliance piece imposed on the customer and the bank. *We're in this together.*

2. Why the bank must comply with it (its legal obligation). *You (the customer and us the bank) are being compelled to do this. If it were up to us, we wouldn't.*

3. Who must comply. *We're not the 'bad guys' here. All the banks have to comply, so it won't help to move banks if you're our customer and reportable.*

4. Who instigated it (government legislation) *We also would like to 'fight the law' but 'the law won'.* Note this one's subtle—but it is implied.

5. Where to go for more information (banking association). *Those guys who manage the whole sector know more than we do. We're like you, an innocent party caught in the system.*

6. How we've done the leg work to make sure we don't bother customers we don't have to. *We're working really hard to make this as hassle free for you as we can. It's the least we can do. We're really sorry we have to do this.*

7. How we're helping you meet the obligations that have been imposed on you (the customer) and on us. *We're in this together. We're on your side and working to help you.*

Also note what we DON'T say here. That's as important as what we do say. We don't mention the billion-dollar penalty to the bank for noncompliance. The change recipients (customers) don't care about that. Banks make billions anyway, which it wouldn't help to remind the customer about. Most people think banks make waaay too much money anyway. Few customers would appreciate the bank trying to overtly play the 'poor me, boohoo, look at my enormous billion-dollar penalty' card. That would really backfire.

Always think carefully through the blow-back on any of your 'what's in it for me' statements. With each WIIFM, think about the recipients and the medium and ask yourself, 'How else could this possibly be interpreted?' For crucial messages, try to test them with a focus group first. This saves an enormous amount of potential public embarrassment and damage control later.

The best outcome you can deliver for a 'project cat food' is that the change flies under the radar. No news is good news on these. Adoption looks good when there's a lack of fanfare. You want hardly a ripple in the pool. If this happens, you've managed to create acceptance of the scale of the negative consequence. In this case, it's not about making people happy or fist pumping about the change; it's all about acceptance or at least quiet resignation!

These projects often carry significant reputational risk if you don't finesse them right. On these, you don't want to make headlines. We were grateful when our bank didn't get a grilling on national radio. Two other banks did, and it was brutal. We also got positive feedback from customers we had to report. Some of these customers wrote in to thank us for our excellent communications. That's because we took the time and considerable effort to draft letters that explained exactly what the customer obligation was in a range of scenarios and what to do about it. Always stating clearly, of course, that the bank was not in a position to provide legal advice and when the bank recommended the customer seek this professional legal advice. Some of those letters went upwards of fifteen drafts and had to go through the project team, marketing, legal, finance, risk, privacy and security, and an external law firm. It was a lot of effort, but the positive public relations was worth it in spades. This is a good example of how to turn a negative into a positive.

How to build the change impact assessment and validate your WIIFMs

You have a range of options for how you compile your change impact assessment. Best case is to run a workshop (or if it's a big piece, a series of workshops), bringing in key stakeholders. In the session, run your stakeholders through a high-level summary of what's changing. Do this in story form. It usually works best to tell the story as a process. Then highlight to participants what the key change points are. Do this based on feedback you've received from previous stakeholder conversations. If you do this well, the feedback will flow. You are checking what you've already understood from sessions held before the workshop. You are also seeking consensus on what you've understood. Workshops are as much about seeking consensus as they are about generating output.

You can have stations on the walls where participants put up post-it notes on charts. These capture what they think are the key change points. Then grade them against an impact scale (low, medium, high).

I have seen a lot of criteria used to quantify the threshold between a low, medium, and high scale of impact. I've not come across a perfect resolution to this question, as there is an unavoidable element of subjectivity to it. You can get into situations where one stakeholder may assess an impact as a high to very high impact, while another may see that same impact as low. This is all dependent on the risk appetite of the person or group assessing the impact. And the accuracy of their grasp on the particulars of what is changing.

Note that the cultural set of an organisation will also influence how small or great they judge the scale of impact to be. Naturally risk-adverse organisations will tend to rate the scale of impact on the high end. Organisations more wired to embrace opportunity will tend to rate on the low end. Watch out for both of these extremes. It will take ongoing stakeholder engagement and qualification of what is really changing to level the perception of the scale of impact to one that approaches reality.

One way of avoiding these more extreme perceptions is to define the level of change impact according to the hours of learning the key stakeholder group will require to move to the future state. In this case, the scale of impact can be defined like this.

1. Low impact depends on no more than one hour or less of learning.
2. Medium impact depends on one to three hours of learning.
3. High impact depends on five hours or more of learning.

I've found this way of quantifying the scale of impact to be a lot less contestable. This helps avoid situations where, say, a general manager thinks the overall impact to operational processes is quite low, but their operational team has graded it as a high impact! The organisational level that an impact assessor operates at can be another big determinant of how high they will perceive the scale of impact to be. I've found there is a lot of variance in people's perception of how much a business change will impact processes and behaviours overall, so you must be prepared to work harder to qualify these aspects accurately.

Subjectivity in rating the change impact level is of course higher near the beginning of the project. As the project proceeds and assumptions are validated, the change impact rating must become more and more accurate. This is why the change impact assessment must be revisited every couple of months.

You can do your assessment workshops remotely using collaborative tools like Microsoft Whiteboard and Miro. The trickiest scenario is when you have attendees both in the room and remotely. Individual workbooks are a good option in this case. That stops virtual participants from twiddling their thumbs during exercises.

If you're super organised and have a creative bent, develop a Lean Canvas. Use this to step participants through the summary of the key change points. Then get them to add their comments and impact ratings and pass on (or collate at the end of the session).

Do your first cut of the change impact assessment as soon as possible. Don't do this alone or with your project manager. The assessment must come from your four key stakeholder groups: change initiators, change partners, change recipients, and change onlookers. It can be helpful to bring together stakeholders who will hold disparate views. This can be about what the biggest impacts are and/or the scale of impact. This is ideal if you're a strong facilitator who can manage the dynamic. If you have these stakeholders in the room together, it will keep the change honest. This means the project doesn't 'mark its own homework'. When that happens, conclusions can be wrongly drawn that the change is low impact to all groups, or high impact to all groups, or everyone welcomes the change. These are all unlikely.

Sometimes, relations between stakeholders are too acrimonious to bring them together. This happens more often than is ideal. Do these groups separately. But play back the compiled impact ratings for feedback from all groups. Agreed impacts and their scale can be quite a negotiation.

If you DO manage to bring the groups together, you can generate what I call 'creative struggle'.[6] I'll talk more about creative struggle in chapter 7. I believe it's the happiest place for the change manager to operate. It has been said that it is the mark of true intelligence to hold two opposed ideas in the mind at the same time, and still retain the ability to function.[7] This is how you exercise the art of the constructive compromise. This is how you get stakeholders with different views to engage in dialogue. If you want to be a successful change manager, you want to embrace this concept. But prepare to hold more than two opposed ideas in the mind at the same time! Here are some great interdepartmental juxtapositions. I suggest these combinations will generate some 'creative struggle'.

- sales and marketing with finance
- product development with legal and risk management
- customer experience with operations management or information technology
- communications and engagement with compliance, assurance, and regulation

We need to respect people's agency or sovereignty in this process. That means we must accept that different roles and departments have different drivers. Those roles attract different skills and personalities. Invite into the conversation those with differing skills and temperaments. That's the creative struggle. You need it to get to the heart of change. Unskilful change managers avoid this. It's labelled 'resistance'. Change initiators may try to shut it down. That's when 'listening' turns to 'telling'.

I realise I'm asking a lot here, in an era where everyone seems to trade off the right to be offended. So, use it judiciously. Don't expose yourself or your participants to exchanges without psychological safety. Culture and the attitude of your sponsor and project or programme manager are big factors in how much of this you can do. But recognise that the best outcomes are forged in dynamic environments. If everyone's 'playing nice' six months out from your go-live, that's not good. Then it's likely the true heart of change will rear its ugly head at delivery. Better to have the creative struggle NOW than on day one of the change.

WIIFMs enable the change

To round this crucial chapter off, let's examine why the WIIFMs are so important. They mean everything. Getting change to stick is about permission, NOT control. Through great WIIFMs, you create conditions that permit change. That permission comes from within each individual. Everyone must choose for themselves. This respects the agency of each individual to determine their future and how they 'play' in it.

Great WIIFMs help people to make informed choices. WIIFMs give them a reason to go beyond the barriers of status quo 'safety' and reach for the gain. Something in the future state that is worth striving for.

You can't make people adopt the change. You can only create conditions that help each individual to want to choose the change. They decide to adopt the change and make it stick. The choice has to be real, meaningful, and emotionally resonant for each individual. The risks must be called out clearly, so the individual makes an informed choice. As a change manager, you are a custodian of the permission to change.

Summary

That's the end of chapter 4. Now that you've finished this chapter, you should understand

- how to structure a change impact assessment,

- what to put in a change impact assessment,

- how to capture a change impact assessment,

- the importance of the gap statement in the change management assessment, and

- how to write good WIIFMs: those that flesh out your change gap statements; those that elicit an emotional resonance; those that compel.

The core message of this chapter is that each point of change needs a meaningful reason to make it stick. The permission to change lies within each individual. Create great conditions for people to choose change. Respect the individual's right to self-determination. No change manager MAKES people adopt the change. They surface the conditions that mean people choose adoption for themselves.

In the next chapter, we'll look at how to shape up your key change actions and deliverables into a solid delivery approach.

CHAPTER 5

Build up from a Base and
Keep it Simple

We're into the guts of the approach. Now we can start thinking about the shape of the ongoing effort to make sure the change sticks. Let's look at what's first.

Where to start your change effort and how to build a great change plan

Right now, change management is in a 'so hot right now, that change management' phase. That's a good thing. But it also comes with a proliferation of giant methodologies. Super complex terminology is required. Also a certain elitism that pervades in some change management circles. This is counter to the work. Or, as a mate of mine once put it, 'Anyone can be a decent change manager if they have some common sense, can read people, and like to get stuff done.' Amen to that. I've been a change manager for thirty years and I've never heard it said better.

Change managers come from all walks of life. They are business analysts and product managers. Sometimes, they are communications managers and engagement specialists. Also, project managers and people seconded onto projects from all walks of life. Never ever think you're not good enough, clever enough, or special enough to do the work of the change manager. You are—and the fact that you even ask the question shows you are. Because good change managers are self-aware people. They are at the growing edge of possibility. Where there's maybe some discomfort, but also a lot of opportunity. And they like it there.

So, first things first. Here's what you must do to be an effective change manager in your own work practice.

1. Get on the ground as quickly as possible. Start sussing things out. That means don't take the word of whoever hired you or seconded you on to the project.

2. Go and talk to people.

3. Ask the same question a lot of times. (Not so people know you're repeatedly asking it, of course. Be a bit stealthy about it!)

4. Suss out who talks straight and who's got too many agendas to be honest. Are the people who have the agendas even aware they have them? Why are those agendas there? What's driving them? Remember, there's often a bunch of unconscious bias due to the kind of roles people have and the organisations people work in. Risk people, well, they tend to be risk adverse, right? They value safety, security, and the avoidance of harm! Sales and marketing people tend to be a bit gung-ho. They value opportunity and excitement.

5. Understand ALL the agendas and why they are there. What is the movement toward gain and away from pain driving each agenda?

6. What is the project actually going to do? Remember, outcomes, not widgets. Outcomes with heart. Things that move people toward gain and away from pain. Keep in mind

people's definitions of pleasure and pain are quite different. Think about someone in risk management. Then think about someone in sales and marketing. Or maybe a customer buying life insurance versus a customer buying the newest hot computer game. The things they would run toward and away from look quite different.

There is a bunch of tools that can be useful to use on the fly to help. My preferred methodologies are 'postage stamp' methods. The temperature check is one you might like to use once you've got to step six above.

How to apply a temperature check exercise

Before you take a temperature check, you need to get an early sense of what the project's doing. You need to know the project's why, who the main stakeholders are, and what they want. Then it's time for a quick temperature check. For each of your key stakeholder groups, draw a line. Say, for example, these are your groups.

- finance team
- HR team
- internal customers
- operations
- external customers

Plot an 'x' somewhere on the line where you've gauged each group is, in terms of receptivity to the change. You can write some notes around the outside about what's holding them back or what the valid objections are. Then you want to formulate your solutions.

Not good at all.   Couldn't be better.

Example: Sense check

Revisit this temperature check periodically throughout the change delivery. You can use it with your stakeholders in focus groups. You can also use it to gauge mood in group dynamics. If the project dynamic is healthy, you can get groups to collectively put an 'x' on the line and then have a group discussion about where the patterns are and why.

I don't recommend this if the group dynamic is more toxic. That would be too confronting and stir up reactivity.

How to apply a stakeholder heat map

Another quick sense-making exercise is the stakeholder heat map. This helps you see how each stakeholder group relates to the others. This is a graph on which you plot your stakeholders against 'x' and 'y' axes. I prefer the version where 'x' equals the stakeholders' level of influence on the project outcomes and 'y' equals the scale of impact of the change to that stakeholder group.

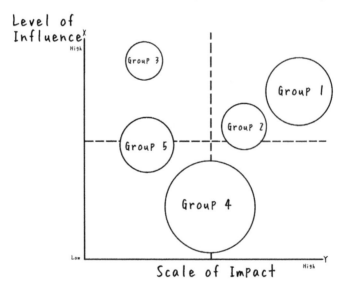

To enhance the richness of the heat map, I like to modify the size of each stakeholder group circle to reflect the relative size of the group. This is shown in the sample heat map above. The biggest stakeholder group you have, by the number of its members, will be the biggest circle. You can also use a colour code to differentiate group clusters, such as internal and external stakeholders. Simple visual keys like this can add an enormous amount of additional insight to your change collateral.

You can do the temperature check and the stakeholder heat map once you've got your first cut of the change impact assessment.

The change plan

After the change impact assessment, you're ready to develop a change plan. There are many schools of thought about a change plan. I've read plans in PowerPoint more than eighty pages long, and Word documents of about fifteen pages. If your project is of any reasonable size—by cost more than $250 thousand and anything up to twenty million—you will need a change plan. My current view is that it shouldn't be more than thirty pages. If it is, you need to roll it up into some more summarised, less detailed statements.

Often you get asked to do a change strategy. This is superfluous in environments where the change approach is already prescribed. In my view, a change strategy should run through the potential options to solve for your change, as in, 'You could do it this way OR you could do it that way.' It then considers the pros and cons of those options and makes a recommendation. If there are no strategic choices to be made, there's no reason to have a change strategy. If you already know that communications will happen in these ways, by these 'voices', via these channels, then you only need to plan when and what. The strategic 'how' has already been answered.

It's the same if learning is delivered by a prescribed team using a prescribed application and channels. The strategic 'how' of shaping up your learning is already specified if you already know these things. You just need the 'what' and 'when' change plan. If you do need a change strategy, that's all good; just check that it adds real value. Worse, don't write a change plan and then call it a strategy or vice versa.

A good change plan should have the following elements.

1. Project overview: This must include why you're doing it. Here are some common reasons:

   - Replace end-of-life system moving out of support,
   - Launch new product to gain market share and increase profit,
   - Reframe the way a service is delivered,
   - Merge two companies,
   - Operationalise a new regulatory requirement,
   - Operationalise a new internal policy and/or a legal or government legislative requirement,
   - Standardise and systematise a process model.

2. Summary of the impact: What groups are impacted? What are their numbers and locations?

3. How much impact to each group (high, medium, low). Chapter 3 includes a way to size the change impact looking at hours of learning required. Perhaps you have a different model. Often you have no choice but to use the agreed organisational approach.

4. Aspects of the change: How many of the ten aspects are changing? The ten aspects of change are

   1. processes,
   2. systems,
   3. tools,
   4. job roles,
   5. critical behaviours,
   6. mindsets, attitudes and/or beliefs,
   7. reporting structure,

8. performance reviews,

9. compensation, and

10. location (or environment).[8]

If more than three to four characteristics are changing, it usually means the overall scale of change is high to at least some of your audience. Write a clear paragraph about each aspects, outlining what will be different.

5. A summary diagram on what the change delivers: Should this flow left to right with what's delivered? What's different? What's the end state? (This one covers the full vision when the project is fully adopted.)

6. Principles under which change management will deliver: How closely are you handholding or are you enabling self-management?

7. What's the point of this plan for each key stakeholder group: Why would they read it and what are they going to get out of it?

A table for your change approach—the guts of your plan

I like this table

Change activity	Ensures that	Approach	Key activities	Key artefacts	Required resource	Initiations date— (target is go-live minus x months)	Activity cycle (target is go-live commencement)

Continuing with the change plan elements

8. Your change road map. This shows the timeline to delivery and the relationship between the key activities the change team will undertake.

9. Your key assumptions, risks, and issues. Sets out what must be in place to ensure change success, and the risks and issues that may limit that success.

10. Resourcing. What are the roles and how many, that will assist to deliver the change plan.

11. Success measurement. How the change management effort will measure the success of its activities.

Example: populated change approach table

Here's an example of a change approach table populated to show you what it looks like.

Change activity	Ensures that	Approach	Key activities	Key artefacts	Required resource	Initi-ations date— (target is go-live minus x months)	Activity cycle (target is go-live com-mence-ment)
Com-munica-tions and engage-ment.	The audience is well informed and sup-portive of the change.	Compre-hensive campaigns. Refer to commu-nications plan and calendar.	Focus groups. Site webinars. Senior Leader Briefings.	Comms plan. Comms calendar. Collateral: articles and blogs.	Comms manager. Comms advisor. Corporate affairs liaison.	Target (go-live) minus nine months. Six months for site-specific comms.	Monthly to key stakehold-ers. Executive updates bi-monthly.

			Brown Bag Sessions Town hall Sessions.	Intranet page. Internet page.			Fort-nightly updates to sites from target (go-live minus four months)
Impact assess-ment	The dif-ferences between how things are currently done and how they will be done are fully under-stood and clearly explained to those receiv-ing the change, in a way that makes sense to them and compels adoption.	High-level assessment within three months. Detailed assessment on the vendor and solution selec-tion. Post detailed require-ments develop-ment.	Work-shops with key stake-holder groups. Straw model validated ongo-ing and refreshed. WIIFMs tested ongo-ing with focus groups.	High Level Impact Assess-ment. Detailed impact assess-ment. WIIFM state-ments bank.	Change lead. Change analyst.	Target minus seven months (for initial detailed impact assess-ment).	Tri-monthly refresh.
Learning	etc.						
etc.							

79

Other rows for this table

Other rows I would expect to see in this table, depending on what the change the projects delivers, are as follows.

Service design: to ensure that the processes, procedures, and business rules required for the future state are codesigned with key stakeholder groups (change recipients) and are in place to inform delivery.

Information management: to ensure that all related collateral is appropriately updated or created to support user adoption go-live across all channels. Generally includes information repository updates, internet and intranet updates, new product guides, and marketing collateral.

Leadership advocacy: to ensure that all leaders are equipped with the skills and resources to understand the business benefits and to advocate strongly and consistently for adoption of the change outcomes.

Organisational design: to ensure that all the required roles, reporting lines, organisational structures, payroll, redundancy, and skills and competency development models are in place prior to implementation.

Change advisory group and champions network: to ensure that a network of key stakeholders, subject matter experts (SMEs) and end users codesign the change management effort and assist with its delivery. A change advisory group is set up as a high-level national body. The champions and superusers networks are the on-the-ground, at site, support mechanisms.

Business readiness: to ensure that a clear picture of what the end users require to adopt the change is in place and implemented prior to the go-live transition.

Change reaction management: to ensure that counters to change adoption are heard and mitigated prior to implementation to improve adoption and ensure the business benefits are realised.

Go-live support: to ensure that the go-live is actively supported during the intensive transition period. (Requires project members to be on site.)

BAU transition; to ensure that all aspects of the change are successfully transitioned to the business through business as usual. Requires identified business owners for all implemented elements and a continuous improvement process in place to update what's delivered. Refer to chapter 10 for more detail on BAU transitions.

Embed and sustain approach: to ensure that the change recipients don't devolve back to the legacy state in the months post-implementation. Requires ongoing induction, learning, leadership advocacy, and performance management incentives in place.

Effective delivery of the change plan

Once you've got your change plan, you're starting to get set up for effective delivery. So, to summarise the 'ride or die' change management artefacts you must have, here they are.

1. Stakeholder assessment.
2. Change impact assessment: high level (at the start when you're getting an approximate feel).
3. Change impact assessment: detailed. (This is when you're in detailed development and understand the nitty gritty of each change point.)
4. Change plan.

5. Communication and engagement plan AND communications and engagement calendar.

6. If learning, learning needs analysis and learning plan.

7. If this is an organisational change, then do the following.

   a. Role sizing.

   b. Consultation document.

   c. Themed consultation response summary.

   d. Final decisions document (and all the HR particulars that flow from this, but have a specialist or a team of specialists on this piece).

   e. If it's a big piece, you need a skills and competencies model.

These are the hard-core deliverables. Everything else I believe is optional. Of course, it depends on the size of your project and team. Anything beyond this could detract from the time you spend with your stakeholders. That's where you should be. That's where you listen, learn, test, influence, and enable. That's the road to change adoption. That's how you make the change stick.

One red flag

Recently I worked on a very large-scale programme. Most of the change management artefacts were captured in giant spreadsheets. This is a red flag. This means you're lost in the woods and can't see the trees. Spreadsheets are for data objects. They break things down into component parts. Change managers must be adept at reading the map of the human heart. Nobody ever found the key to the human heart in a spreadsheet. Did you pay close attention to chapter

3? Then you know that the real key is emotional resonance with what the change delivers.

Spreadsheets have their place—they're great for logistics and capturing complexity in its constituent parts. But spreadsheets are about fixity, and literally are 'the Matrix'; human hearts are about fluidity. The human heart defies 'the Matrix'. Spreadsheets 'break down things' but your change approach must 'build up things'. There's no story in a spreadsheet. But change is always a relational story. Your key artefacts must reflect this.

Change Cat knew... the answer is in the conversation, NOT the spreadsheet!

Another red flag

Here's another relevant story from the giant public sector programme from a few years back. (This programme was the example I
used for why I had to get out in the first chapter.) One day, I got into
the elevator on the top floor with one of the lead IT guys. He was
on a foundation project that was a key enabler to the other four big
projects in the programme. We rode down from the top floor to the
ground without anyone else getting in. There were loads of reports
and spreadsheets flying around about that project at the time. All
those reports reported green. That's 'green for good' and 'green for
go'. When we stepped in that lift and the doors closed, I glanced over
at … let's call him *Bill*. Bill looked tired. Skin tone was grey and his
eyes were bloodshot. The slope of his shoulders was dejected. We
faced the lift doors side by side (as you do) and I asked, low key,
'Hey, Bill, how's it going?'

He paused (pauses speak louder than words if you're listening).
Then he looked slowly and dejectedly skyward. Time lengthened. We
rode several more floors in silence.

'A few issues?' I enquired gently.

He exhaled slowly and looked at the ceiling one more time. 'Yep,
a few issues, Barb,' he said.

I gave him a conciliatory smile, then the elevator doors sighed
open, and we went about our day.

After that encounter, I made some further low-key enquiries with
other people I knew on that project. The news wasn't good. From that
point on, I began to surface on my change report that there were some
challenges to delivery. Knock-on effects to the programme would
require careful management. I didn't know if too much attention was
paid to what the change lead was reporting on that giant programme
of work. When that project failed to deliver, there was a lot of falling
about and gnashing of teeth from senior management. Why didn't
they know sooner they railed?! The reality was there to be read all

along. It always is if you have eyes to see and ears to hear and a heart to empathise and attune.

Be a truth teller

The environment constantly communicates the health of the change state. But you have to stop, listen, and feel the project pulse to read it. You also have to stop drinking the project Kool-Aid. In my experience, the bigger the programme is, the more Kool-Aid there is to drink. Don't be a lotus eater—be a truth-teller—remember chapter 1 and your values. If you believe in the project, look for opportunities to land the truth of the change state. But do this in ways that will be heard to best effect.

Develop your key documents as quickly as possible. This is part of early traction. Stakeholders tend to be most anxious at the start of a project. Particularly senior ones, your change initiators. Then do them again shortly before go-live. The sooner you can articulate the key points of the change—Who? When? How? What? Why?—then the closer to the mark you'll hit to achieve high adoption and make the change stick.

The greatest change manager of all is time. Warm people up to the idea of your change as quickly as possible. You'll start to see shift toward the change adoption in a three to six-month period.

Another large-scale programme

Further back in my career, I worked within another large-scale programme. One nationwide bank was acquired by another. Internally, this acquisition was euphemistically called the 'integration programme'. Actually, it was more like the scene at the end of the original *Fantastic Voyage* movie. That's when a crew and a spaceship are shrunk down and injected into the blood stream of a dying patient to save them. At the end of the movie, a character is trapped in the viewing bubble at the top of the spaceship. They are consumed, head-first, by a pitiless white blood cell.

The 'Acquiring Bank A' was very smart about it. They took ten years to 'absorb' the 'Acquired Bank B'. They kept 'Bank B's' well-known and much-loved marketing image, colours, and logos. They took 'Bank B's' internet banking app and made it the standard. It had the better look and feel, plus superior features and functionality. 'Bank B' was much better at customer service and had an intensely loyal customer base. 'Bank A' was shrewd enough to know not to throw out the baby with the bank water. They assimilated all the best attributes of 'Bank B' into their own model. They had to integrate all the IT, so they also did their core banking replacement early, years before any of the other banks in the market did it. Today, they're the leading bank in the country, with the biggest market share.

Ten years after the acquisition, 'Bank A' finally got rid of 'Bank B's' branding and logo. One by one, they closed their branches. This happened without even a whimper, let alone a bang.

Time is the best change manager of all. Humans are adaptive creatures. In ten years, what was thought unthinkable became 'normal'. Remember, the future state is just the current state a little bit ahead of today.

The other factor, which, if you're on this type of project you shouldn't discount, is customer inertia. I know because I was a long-term customer of 'Bank B'. I strongly disliked the 'big corporate' image of 'Bank A'. But, did I defect? No. I had a range of accounts set up and fine-tuned over many years. Also, I'd got used to their internet banking features. Did I shop around looking for similar accounts with a different bank I liked more? Hell, no! Did I moan about it? Hell, yes!

Now we're back to one of our basic formulas. People move toward gain and away from pain. The pain of being a customer of a bank whose brand image I wasn't fond of was less than the pain (time and inconvenience) of moving all my accounts to another bank.

Sometimes you get people to adopt a change when you reality check with them that it's 'the lesser of two evils'.

A word on 'agile'

Change managers work more often now on 'agile' projects. Or, in my experience, more commonly 'wagile'. That's a hybrid term to describe agile development with waterfall delivery. You must work in incremental segments anchored to the focus of each sprint cycle in these cases. It's easy to deliver in sprint increments when you're talking software. These increments often work less well for large-scale people impact change. People want to see the whole map of the change before they can see themselves in it. Therefore, it's very hard to deliver significant people change in a full agile model. If you're really going gangbusters, you can get your change plan down to a Lean Canvas A3 of a couple of pages.

I suspect the local corporate market has a bit of work to do to catch up to less being more in documentation. Especially in the public sector. But it's coming.

If you're wondering what should be on that Lean Canvas, again, it's about doing the basics well. I would cover

1. What's changing: widget level.
2. What's changing: outcome level.
3. Key stakeholders impacted, numbers, and locations.
4. Key stakeholders' perception of change.
5. Which of the ten aspects of change are affected and the scale of impact to each. These ten aspects are listed in this chapter in 'The change plan' section.
6. Roadmap and timeline for change activities.
7. Governance—key players and team members.
8. Key risks and issues.

Summary

That's the end of chapter 5. This chapter covers how to 'peg out' your change management effort. You understand the 'ride or die' collateral. That's the collateral you must have for success. And you understand the key subject matter you need to cover in each document.

The core message of this chapter is to keep it simple. Your change approach and collateral should be easy to use and understand. Don't create an approach that acts as a barrier between yourself and your real customers. You can't know your stakeholders if your nose is always in a spreadsheet. To deliver change that sticks, walk a mile in the recipients' shoes. Then walk the road beside them all the way. You've got to get out from behind the keyboard to do that. And the answer definitely isn't in the spreadsheet.

In the next chapter we'll explore how to work with the attitudinal, behavioural, and belief sides of change.

CHAPTER 6

Black Arts and Dark Ops

Approaches to delivering successful behavioural change tend to break into two camps. Camp one acts as if behavioural change, let's call it 'mindset shift', is 'all the things'. This change manager tends to focus the majority of the effort on the behavioural pieces. In these cases, there's an enormous amount of focus on 'the feeling of the pain'. This change manager is a huge empath. A pulsing, undulating sponge of emotional availability.

In contrast, camp two ignores that the behavioural change is even a thing. The assigned change manager tends to be less emotionally available. This time it's all about the facts, quantitative data, and—uh—spreadsheets.

Understanding the basics of delivering successful behavioural change

In my view, neither of these approaches has the high ground. If you make the project all about the emotions, the change work stream becomes too self-indulgent. It fails to get traction. It bogs down in a big emotional wallow. Suddenly you have a big love fest of 'listening deeply' to the stakeholders. But to what end? A project delivery change manager must 'feel the pain' in service to achieve outcome. Empathy isn't an end in itself. Yet, if you ignore the emotional reality of the change, one thing is certain. You just 'turned up the dial' on getting widgets only. *Nice widgets, shame about the low adoption.* Neither is the way.

Often smart, highly analytical, and very bottom-line oriented people occupy the change initiator role. They call the shots on what gets focussed on. They also dictate who gets hired. This is a trap, as 'like hires like'. Highly analytical, detailed change initiators hire mirrors of themselves. They use change managers who speak as they do and act as they do. They need to hire their opposite. They need more emotionally aware people. They need change managers who are highly people attuned. But it must be attunement in service to change adoption.

Sometimes the highly analytical, return-on-investment-focussed types can get spooked. They have a brush with the 'scary' emotional response to the change. For example, the union gets a whiff of it and comes on strong. Maybe an initial briefing with internal teams doesn't go well—it didn't get positioned right. Maybe something got leaked to the media at an inopportune time before all the ducks were in a row. This can cause a knee-jerk response.

Then the 'pulsating emotional sponge' type of change manager gets hired. They're labelled 'the custodian of all things emotional and icky'. That's not ideal and may in fact lead to a worse outcome than if the change manager role is left vacant. That's harsh, but the pain can't JUST 'be felt'. It must be felt to be understood. Then you move it to a new state. Protracted 'feeling the pain' keeps the change recipients stuck in the pain, stuck in the fear of the future state. Pain must be felt to build a constructive way forward. Then empathy is in the service of delivering change that sticks.

Research shows it takes six seconds to sit with a difficult emotion before it begins to move to a new state.[9] That's not a lot to ask. But you have to sit with it with the intent to move it rather than to stay stuck with it. What matters is what's beyond the pain and fear.

The ideal change manager operates somewhere in the middle ground. You listen, you empathise, you strategise, and then you enable a way forward. Away from pain, toward gain. You shine a light on the path to adoption and the benefits it brings.

So, let's look at how you understand what mindset shifts your change needs to make it stick.

First, do your initial interviews. Then develop your stakeholder analysis and change impact assessment. These will tell you plenty. See the list of likely inevitable tensions in a workshop, as outlined in chapter 3. The current mindsets will be on full display in these sessions. Change managers must read a room. It is an essential skill. You tend to read more about this talent in books about the psychology of selling. But it's equally applicable to the profession of change management.

Research shows that the impression you make on people is 7 percent what you say, 38 percent your tone of voice and 55 percent how you look when you say it.[10] Your stakeholders will tell you everything about their attitudes, beliefs, and behaviours. You just have to notice it.

While they talk, where are their eyes going? Who do they glance at? How reluctant or keen are they to speak? Who dominates in the room? Who looks for acceptance from others in the room and why? Who talks too much? Who doesn't talk enough? Who's talking the talk but not walking the walk? Who's a keyboard warrior? Who never turns up to meetings and why is that? Are they super capable but horribly overcommitted? Or are they a poster child for presenteeism? You need to know the answer to these key questions.

There are cues too many to mention that alert you to stakeholder mindsets. The dynamics of your change can be read in every single meeting and every single glance.

A large acquisition example

When I was starting out, I worked on a large acquisition programme. An established Australasian insurance company bought a 'best of British' investment management company. I worked in the information management part of the programme. The first thing they did was to build a knowledge management system. This was to integrate the diverse wisdom and experience of these two organisations. At the time, I was seconded to London. Not to keep you in suspense, the acquisition failed. Years later, the eye-watering figure of the write-down appeared in the Australasian press.

However, the writing was on the wall from the start. The temperaments, skills, and personalities of the two organisations were completely at odds. They both operated in the financial services industry, but that's where the similarities ended. They weren't a good fit for each other. The insurance business was an aggressive operator. It was filled with hard-eyed actuaries, intent on calculating odds. Those odds ensure house wins enough to make a profit and continue writing more insurance business. The rest of the organisation was an army of claims processors and support functions. They were trained to follow highly prescribed processes to the letter. Insurance companies incentivise claim assessors to find all the valid reasons NOT to pay out. They also do volumes and sell to 'the average man on the street'. There are no prizes for higher-than-average claim payouts. Insurers clinically assess odds to minimise the threat of payout. Their bread and butter is home and contents insurance and car insurance. It is a low-entry, high-volume business pitched to the average person on the street. The sales spiel is 'financial peace of mind for the average person'.

In contrast, let's look at the 'best of British, old-school, blue blood' fund manager that was the other organisation. This operated in an elitist, class based 'old Etonian' world. It also played the odds, but it played in the deep end of opportunity. Calculated opportunity. Their value proposition was based on high-value and high-entry threshold, low-volume and high-return business. The insurance company catered to the working and middle class. The fund manager catered to the high wealth upper class market. The hire pool for each organisation couldn't have been more different. The insurance company rolled from 'you have to hang on to your money to make money'. The other was about 'spend money to make money'. I hope you can see here that one of these things is not like the others. The two couldn't have been more different in terms of the people they hire, the work they do, their values, and the client base they cater to.

The attitudes of employees in these companies were diametrically opposed. Deeply incompatible. Their personal and professional drivers were at odds. It was inevitable, on reflection, that the merger wouldn't work.

I was exposed to this experience pretty early on in my career when I was relatively green. I also worked on the information rather than change management side of things. That they chose to lead the integration of the two disparate organisations by developing an information management repository speaks volumes. Surfacing great information counts for nothing if the behaviours of the users aren't aligned to realise the value. In this case, the behavioural change to align the employees' values and drivers was never addressed, nor I believe even really acknowledged. This is back to chapter 1 and how everything needs to flow from our values. Values alignment applies equally to something as big as an organisation.

I've often wondered if this could have been more successful. The funds management firm could have been acquired but still run as a separate enterprise. Electronic alerts could have flagged cross-selling opportunities. But only when a crossover was beneficial. This keeps the skills, competencies, and mindsets of the employees discrete.

The moral of the tale

The example above is an extreme one. But the moral of the tale runs true. Any change effort must first establish how compatible it is with the values and behaviours of the impacted parties. Do the skills, temperaments, and mindsets of the change recipients align? Do they support adoption of the change? The bigger the gap, the harder it will be to make the change. Not impossible. But you need a clear conversation with senior leaders if the gap is wide. One that calls out how big that gap is and what it will take to bridge it. How many people are you prepared to swap out, or even could you? Or is this a non-negotiable change? Have things really got to a point that the organisation has to shed employees to stay afloat? Has a conversation with those employees happened to explore alternatives? Is there a prospect of large-scale redundancy, and if there is, how aligned to the organisation's professed culture and values is this option?

A new house

Here's a different story about completely missing the behavioural gap. A couple of years ago, we built a new house. We were very excited to move in and start using all the lovely new appliances. But we got a bit stumped the first time we came to stack the dishwasher. Where was the cutlery basket we asked, scratching our heads? There was this weird pull-out tray at the top, with a row of grills and notches on it. We couldn't fathom what that was for. We pored through the manual but couldn't see anything about it. *How weird*, we thought. *Did the manufacturer forget to include the cutlery basket?* We resorted to dumping all the cutlery in this weird top tray with all the grills in it. Everything was all piled up on each other. Nothing ever got fully clean in there, but we got used to it.

After we'd been in the house almost a year, a good friend of mine came to stay. Someone who loves a good appliance, she helped to stack the dishwasher on her first night. *Ah, you've got one of these new cutlery trays*, she said with satisfaction. We watched, mystified, as she proceeded to lay our cutlery sideways in the tray. She neatly slotted the tops and bottoms of each item into the individual grooves. None of us quite had the bottle to admit we'd had no idea that was what it was for!

This is where the lesson on behavioural change comes in. Project teams often deliver new-fangled things. The project team can easily get so used to the promise of the future state that it becomes 'normal' FOR THEM. So much so that they forget how much the future state differs from normal for the user. That's because the project team has already adopted the change. They forget the change recipient is still way back behind them, oblivious to this new future.

In the dishwasher example, the current state was for cutlery to go in a basket, facing upright, at the bottom of the dishwasher. This was our user expectation. The future state was each item placed sideways in a pull-out tray at the top of the dishwasher. It's a big difference. So, you have to explain the change in a very clear and explicit way. You also have to explain the benefit. From a user adoption perspective, it wasn't a great change. It's easy to chuck a bunch of cutlery into a stand-up basket. A lot less finicky than placing each item separately horizontally in a pull-out tray.

It still rankles to have to place each piece in this darned tray. The kids just fling things in, close the door, and hope for the best. No great movement toward gain and away from pain here. Actually, the reverse! The future state is more of a pain than the current. Behaviours haven't been accounted for here to get the change to stick.

The dishwasher example above shows how behavioural change hides in plain sight. That's why you must do walk-throughs with key users. You need a cross-section of your change recipients to come in. Then walk them through all the changes. Their feedback, overt and covert, uncovers the behavioural changes.

New ways of working: A case study with Suze

Another example is the common theme I see lately around 'new ways of working' (given the abbreviation of NWOW) or just 'ways of working' (WOW). This is usually about changing highly operational, procedure-oriented employees into something completely different. These are employees constrained by strict policies, procedures, and business rules. They are rewarded on through-put volume and case closure in set timeframes. Suddenly, cross-skilled, multi-disciplinarian collaborative teams are 'all the rage'. Ones that work by exception. Lateral thinking and cross team collaboration are the new goals. For these rule-bound and regulated employees, this is a case of 'Toto, we're not in Kansas anymore.'

Let's look at a case study about Suze.

Suze has worked for the organisation for twelve years. She started working as an administrator for the claims officers, then became a junior in the claims department. Now she's a senior claims manager. Her day consists of assessing claim applications, checking against rules to determine eligibility, and sending them off to another team if complex. Most of the time, Suze is a checkpoint that all the information is there and she sends the claim back requesting more information if it's not complete. Suze is also a checkpoint to close claims in the system once completed.

Now the organisation wants to embrace 'new ways of working'. Claims are automatically assessed. The majority are auto approved. Suze's job will now be to intervene on claims that can't be approved or declined automatically. Suze has new delegations. She's told to use lateral thinking skills to work out what is missing from the claim. Then to clean up the claim so that it is either accepted or rejected. So, yesterday, Suze worked in a highly regulated environment. The rules of work were covered in prescriptive policies. These policies were spelled out in detailed processes, procedures, and business rules. Where there was a complex issue, Suze handed the claim off to a specialist team.

She had no delegation. Her performance review revolved around how many claims she had closed in a set period. Now success measurement has shifted to a new measurement of the quality of the care provided for approved claims.

The road is long and full of challenges if you ask for new behaviours of this scale. Particularly from people who were originally hired for a completely different skill set. More so if the new behaviours required are counter to the behaviours you rewarded for a very long time. It's possible, but it takes real commitment. And the best change manager of all is time. Don't lead these changes with impassioned statements about how it's not about redundancy. Or how you want to keep staff and move them into the new model. Particularly if it is about cost-cutting through automation and redundancy. Because, yes, this happens, and it is truly inauthentic. But also because not all your people will want to make the change. Or be capable of making it. Not without long-term, sustained, and invested capability building. You're asking for completely different behaviours which come from different temperaments.

Future-state person is an intuitive, lateral-thinking, calculated risk-taker. Current-state person is the inverse of this. Be clear with your change initiators on the scale of the capability gap in these cases. Your antenna should always twitch when you hear phrases like 'new ways of working'.

Explore the behavioural gap

You can use a variant of your change impact assessment to explore the behavioural gap. It's also useful to do a behavioural change diagnostic. Focus your questions on the emotional response to the change.

Here are some key questions for a behavioural change diagnostic.

- What will be hardest about this change for you and why?
- What's most appealing about the change and why?
- Do you think this change will work?

- What would you need to make it work?
- What do you think would work better and why?
- What do you think leaders haven't considered about this change that they need to know?
- What do you think the skills are you'll need to develop to be successful when things change?
- How do you feel you need to be supported to make this change?

You need to focus questions around what people THINK and FEEL about the change. That helps you understand what they will DO or NOT DO to adopt the change.

Once you've done this, you've found your biggest change hot spots. These hot spots are the points at which it will be hardest to make the change stick. Better yet, you understand why they're hard and what it will take to address them.

Here's the sequence to identify and develop your approach for mindset shift.

- View the change through the end-to-end process view of your change.
- Understand all of the actors at each stage.
- Understand their current attitudes, beliefs, and behaviours.
- Develop powerful WIIFMs that will move recipients toward adoption.
- Look at the status transactions between stakeholders, such as these:
  - ◦ Who has power over whom in any exchange?
  - ◦ Who is most in control and who is least in control?
  - ◦ Which transactions will help make the change stick?
  - ◦ Which transactions will hinder?

- ○ What can you do to minimise the unhelpful transactions and enhance the helpful ones?
- ○ You need to be interrogating yourself on 'Who calls the shots on who here?'
- ○ Whose work derails if another group doesn't support their work?
- ○ What is the attitude of the less dominant party to the status transaction?
- ○ Is it resentful? Most likely it is. How does that resentment show itself?
- ○ How can you intervene to reduce that resentment?

- What are the key influencing conversations you need to have with the change initiators?

- What are the conversations to help them understand the behavioural challenges for the recipients?

- How can you get beyond the alienating platitudes, such as the following?
  - ○ 'We know change is hard.' It's always a lot harder if you start with this one. The leader just shot themselves in the foot right there.
  - ○ 'We know we're asking a lot from you, but we're here to support you.' This one sounds good the first time. However, it plays REALLY BADLY if it's not followed up promptly with the actionable steps to demonstrate what the support is. That support needs to be meaningful, such as, Will we backfill? Will we stagger the roll-out? Will we recruit temporary help to manage any transition backlogs? Will we run a long, end-to-end pilot to make sure everything works well? Or will we pilot with a small pilot unit and then scale?

Explore the behavioural change hot spots

At this point in the delivery cycle, the behavioural change hot spots must be thoroughly identified. Leaders are on board with the scale of the behavioural change. They send the right, authentic messages to their people.

Now it's a matter of careful planning to enable the required transition. There are key elements to it. The change delivery for behavioural change must include these things.

1. Leadership advocacy.

2. Clear policies, processes, procedures, and business rule changes.

3. Realistic delegations.

4. Clear and explicit standard operating procedures.

5. Updates to all channel reference material.

6. Performance management guidance scripts for people leaders.

7. Regular messaging for people leaders.

8. Appropriate team-leader-led break-out activities. These must be scenario based and role specific.

9. Communication articles that celebrate milestones and successes.

10. Case study examples of how people made the change. These cover their struggles and how they overcame them. They call out how proud they are of what they've achieved. Include lots of photos. Short videos are great for this. Stories from the coalface featuring 'real stories, real people' are gold. These are worth ten senior leader impersonal, executive buzz word bingo briefings. Note that if you do happen to have a true servant leader at the helm, roll them out at every available opportunity to point out the North Star you're heading toward.

11. Posters and visual management boards that reinforce the behavioural change. Present this in clear 'soundbite straight

from the horse's mouth' sentences. Pictures do speak a thousand words here.

12. Recruitment and induction materials. These reinforce the new attitudes, beliefs, and behaviours. Screen and score candidates on these attributes.

13. Meaningful incentives. An increase in pay if key performance indicators (KPIs) are met is always compelling (provided they are the right KPIs). There are other perks that can be offered such as product staff discounts, extra staff reward points, tickets to premium sports events and/or shows, and priority options on newly launched goods and services.

14. Champion networks and site specific superusers—pulled from your biggest influencer pool.

Key to number eight

To me, number eight on the list above is the MOST important (but it's number eight in the sequence of activities). It describes how to create effective team leader break-out exercises. Let's work through how to do it well.

Decent learning uses a 'tell, show, do' sequence. You want to script materials for your team leaders to talk about the change and why it's a good thing. This is 'tell'. The 'show' is the celebration of success activities. The 'do' is team exercises in small breakout groups. Groups have scenarios to work through. Each scenario calls on the group to make a core decision. The scenarios are tailored to the particular tasks that each group performs.

The resolution options must cover the following.

1. How we do it in the current state.

2. How we should do it in the future state.

3. Another wild card option.

You ask each team member to decide which approach they would take to resolve a problem. Now here's the most important thing. There's no negative judgement or consequence for getting it wrong. That means no judgement for choosing the current state answer. You want to permit a mindset change. That means you hold a learning space for people to test and learn. People only test and learn in safe environments. It's only when we understand why we're wrong that we can start to choose a new right answer. We need an aha moment. That's when we understand the difference between yesterday's right answer and today's.

Change Cat knew...
to change
behaviours you
need great "ahah"
moments and
excellent treats!

Remember, you only just changed the right answer. People need time and space to catch up. There can't be a penalty here, only encouragement to choose something new and be rewarded for that choice.

A new bank

A while back, I was part of the learning delivery team that launched a new bank in New Zealand. The bank was a new venture set up within the national postal service. I was a learning co-facilitator in the southern region. With a colleague, I fronted a five-day learning course to turn postal workers into bank tellers. No small ask.

On day one of the first five-day course, people milled around nervously. They took time finding seats, talking to neighbours, or rummaging through bags. Sharp on nine o'clock, I said, 'Right,' in a decisive tone to bring the room's attention to me. A semi-circle of faces all jumped. Then, in unison, they all folded their arms.

Oh, boy, here we go, I thought.

I looked round the room and realised I was among a sea of grey hair and spectacles. Employees in the south were long tenured. They worked in smaller, more isolated towns. Ones with few job opportunities. People found jobs, then they stayed. They stayed for decades. Also, it's the postal service, right? One of the last bastions of 'a job for life'. Many of these people had been in their current roles for decades. These people went through the schooling system in the late fifties to early seventies. The school system was different then. Big on discipline, big on conformity, big on 'sit up straight and fold your arms'. Punitive. More about judgement than permission.

I realised my colleague and I were going to have to work very hard. We needed to create an environment that permitted change. An environment in which it was 'okay to choose change'. These folks had been rewarded for decades on how many stamps they sold in a day. Now the organisation required them to chat comfortably with potential banking customers. To be knowledgeable about the bank products to achieve those customers' hopes and dreams.

In that learning room, we needed to provide space for an adoptive mindset. One where there would be more upside to risking something new than to staying the same. This is a HUGE factor in behavioural change. People only put their toe in the water when they're confident you'll help keep them afloat until they can swim.

Changing culture

A key factor to remember in all these situations is how important it is to model the behaviours you want.

My definition of culture is as follows: 'Culture is an organism of collective consciousness. It constantly assesses and interprets complex environmental signals to determine the ways in which it is acceptable and not acceptable to behave.'

It's an amalgam of hair-trigger responsiveness. It's built up from the attitudes, beliefs, and behaviours of every individual. It's a big ask to expect people to become less rule dependent and risk adverse. It's a big ask to expect people to be more creative and adaptive in their work practice if yesterday was the opposite of this. You need to make them feel that it's okay to explore the possibilities. That starts with how you roll when you're with them.

- What do you do when someone gives you feedback?
- What do you do when someone challenges what you say?
- How do you respond when the communication doesn't happen as you'd hoped?
- What about when your PowerPoint won't load?
- The first screen has a glaring typo?
- Or the system goes on the fritz in the middle of the presentation?

If you want people to adopt an adaptive mindset, then you need to show it's safe to do so. In any change scenario, people are constantly asking themselves two questions. They are, 'Yes, but is it safe?' 'If I make this change, will I be rewarded or penalised?'

You must get ahead of the game. Show in every word and deed that, yes, it is safe to change. Next show HOW to change. Finally WHY it's worthwhile to change. And so we're back to our fundamentals again. These are the fundamentals.

1. Make the mindset shift attractive. A move toward gain and away from pain.
2. Make not changing unattractive. How does it increase movement toward pain?
3. Use your breakout exercises to reinforce these points.
4. Ensure leaders reinforce rather than undermine the mindset shift. A common example of undermining the message is when leaders talk effusively in a speech about how open and approachable they are and how much they want to hear the hard issues. Then, when some brave soul raises a hard issue in question time, they shut them down, and even actively undermine them. Everyone is watching and reading the signs in this case. The Magic 8-Ball for change adoption points to 'chances are not good'.

Leveraging the first follower is also powerful. This is where the first celebration of success kicks in. Once one person models the new behaviour, start the celebration. Pick up the story and use it in your communications. Put it in an intranet article. See if you can get the sponsor and/or the top executive to talk about it. Better yet, get employees or customers to talk about it.

Six key lessons for delivering successful attitudinal, behavioural, and belief change

Predominantly, mindset shifts fail for the following reasons.

1. It wasn't the people, they would have made the change fine. But the project wasn't clear about what the change recipients wanted. Projects and sponsors aren't always completely clear on the intent of what they want. So, there's lots of scope for the delivery of something that doesn't fix the root cause issue. Then you can't articulate what the requested behavioural change is.

   Lesson One: Keep your senior leaders clear on the consequence of achieving the future state. They haven't always thought it through all the way sometimes. That's where you come in.

2. Not modelling what you want enough. No performance management of what you don't want. You must have courageous conversations about the behaviours you want and the ones you don't count. Don't think your people are mind-readers.

   Lesson Two: Tell the stories. It's never too early to start.

3. Not giving enough time for people to make the shift.

   Lesson Three: Time is the greatest change manager of all. Let the change become the new norm. You have to let this unfold.

4. Painting the change as highly ambitious and transformational at the start, but falling far short of this in what's actually delivered. Talk needs to become action. Don't 'tell' at this stage. You must 'show' and 'do'.

   Lesson Four: Hold the vision and keep calm under fire.

5. Watch out for leaders changing horses on people midstream. If the change initiators want something different from what was originally intended, then reset. Successful behavioural change delivery takes resilience and patience. Your road map to make the change stick needs to be at least nine months. That's for a mid-sized piece, where at least three of the ten aspects of change listed in chapter 5 are impacted.

   Lesson Five: Keep consistent and keep the faith.

6. Not holding your leaders to full accountability. If they don't do it, nobody will.

   Lesson Six: Leaders lead cultural change 100 percent of the time. Culture is always watching, and culture never sleeps.

The bank set-up in the postal service is one of the biggest behavioural change pieces I've worked on. The ask was to take long-term employees and completely transform them. They operated in a world of closed-ended questions such as, 'How many stamps do you want?' and 'Do you want that parcel tracked?'

Now they were called on to be masters of the open-ended conversation. Asked to have exploratory conversations. Ones that start with phrases such as, 'So, what do you want to achieve in the next couple of years?' 'Tell me about your plans for the future?' 'Tell me your plans for … travel, career, house-buying, starting a family, hobbies, business start-up and expansion.'

I wondered if some of the learners would make the change.

The new bank system technology was another hurdle. I talked to a branch manager at the end of one five-day course about one learner. This person had struggled with the system and not got through a single systems training exercise in five days. The branch manager told me, 'She's one of my best people. She tells me the new system isn't working properly.'

I couldn't help myself and responded, 'Well, most systems don't work when you whack twenty wrong keys in ten seconds.'

There was a pause, then the manager responded, 'Okay, then we need to get her more help when she comes back to the branch.'

I seriously wondered whether this person was capable of making the change. But I was super impressed by her manager's commitment to support her through it. Also, of course, ashamed by what I'd blurted out! I was also curious enough to check back some months later. Lo and behold, this learner was now thriving. She loved the freedom, creativity, and 'value add' in the day of being a banker and doing a 'job that counts'. She had found that selling banking products suited her. They were products that helped people to secure their future.

Of course, whacking keys is a 'fight or flight' type of response to pressure. Fear catalyses people's reactivity. Behavioural change requires safe space. That's where the aha moment happens. It must happen for each individual in an unforced way. You can't force behavioural change to happen. You CAN enable the conditions to make it an attractive choice.

People in a state of high reactivity can't learn, let alone change. Remember that.

All change interventions to effect behavioural change must be spacious. Leave room for people to breathe.

In this case, the organisation gave their staff the time and support to make the transition. The attrition rate nationally was remarkably low, given the size of the change gap. The target number of start-up customers was reached in a time that far exceeded expectations. That bank is still thriving and growing today.

These pieces are always about developing a transaction in trust. The person undergoing the change must be coaxed and encouraged, given time to permit themselves to adapt to the change.

Finally, you won't ever get all of the people to make the change all of the time. Attrition rates will vary, but there will be those who self-select to opt out. You should always allow for about 30 percent of people to not want to make the journey with you—and that's okay. This sort of contingency planning must be discussed with senior stake-holders. It needs to happen early so there are 'no surprises down-stream'. This may mean the need for backfill or short-term hire during the transition period.

Summary

That's the end of chapter 6. Now you have the high-level playbook for mindset change. You have learnt the six key lessons for successful mindset shift.

> **Lesson One:** *Keep your senior leaders clear on the consequence of achieving the future state. They haven't always thought it through all the way sometimes. That's where you come in.*
>
> **Lesson Two:** *Tell the stories. It's never too early to start.*
>
> **Lesson Three:** *Time is the greatest change manager of all. Let the change become the new norm. You have to let this unfold.*
>
> **Lesson Four:** *Hold the vision and keep calm under fire.*
>
> **Lesson Five:** *Keep consistent and keep the faith.*
>
> **Lesson Six:** *Leaders lead cultural change 100 percent of the time. Culture is always watching, and culture never sleeps.*

The core message of this chapter is that mindset shift takes time and tenacity. You can't force people to change their mindset. They have to decide to choose it for themselves. Set up plenty of aha moments for people to experience what the required change is. Be clear on the value of it TO THEM. People need to see others do it, then to experience the difference themselves. They need frequent opportunities to try the new things in a safe space. Reward the early adopters. Tell their stories.

In the next chapter we look at how to handle any sudden course corrections.

CHAPTER 7

Heading Roadblocks off at the Pass

There is a term in Hakomi, a psychotherapy modality, called 'creative struggle'. Some time ago I went to a daylong workshop with a master Hakomi practitioner. She asked for a volunteer to come forward and curl up in a ball on hands and knees. I volunteered and scrunched myself up as small as I could. The practitioner asked for several volunteers to come and gently press their hands on my back and shoulders. I was then instructed to 'unfold'. I did this gradually, using the pressure of the hands to coax me into new positions. Sometimes I turned into the strongest pressure, and sometimes I resisted, choosing my own new shape. Inside I was asking, *What are we doing? What's this for? What's happening next? When will this end?*

When the process finished, I was fully upright. I felt a profound sense of peace. The practitioner, who knew how to listen, observe, and wait—just wait—said after a long silence, 'What are you?'

I said, without thinking, 'I'm a sunflower … turning to the sun.'

There was a collective ah from the group. In that moment, I felt the truth of that statement. All the pressure of that time, my work life, my flat situation, my worries and fears fell away. I was a sunflower turning to the sun. Simple—doing what it's meant to.

Dealing with the barriers to change adoption

It was years later before the full import of that exercise came to me. Shortly after that experience, I made a series of profound changes in my life. I moved house, left a relationship, and changed roles. At the time, I wasn't consciously aware of the connection. It was only looking back later that I realised how profound that moment had been. It helped me to experience a simplicity and clarity in my life I hadn't felt for a long time. It was a sign pointing the way. It reminded me of where I wanted to go and what I wanted to do.

Leading people through change is like this. A change of state is introduced into the environment. Everyone must 'push' against that change. They unfold toward the change or they recoil. Each individual has a different appetite for the 'creative struggle'. Some yield and some recoil.

I'm telling this story as a counter to the common label of any change opposition as 'change resistance'. Change resistance has become quite the thing in the last decade. It's a focus of much change management literature these days. I would suggest that what is happening is 'creative struggle'. A change unfurling before our eyes. The birth of something new. It's often a little painful, at least at first. Not that easy, not that simple, and a little confrontational. That's what growth is.

To go back to my example of the post office employees transforming into front line banking staff, imagine the internal 'creative struggle' that everyone had to go through there. The soul-searching and self-doubt. The confrontation to make peace with what was being asked of them.

Imagine that internal dialogue as the learners sat down for the first day of learning. It would have been something like this:

> 'I've been selling stamps and doing motor vehicle registration for twenty-three years. How am I going to be a banker?'

> 'I've never really used a computer before. What's this going to look like?'

'What if I'm not good enough?'

'What if I'm the only one who can't do it?'

'What if I lose my job?'

'What will my colleagues think of me if I can't do it?'

'What if I'm too old for this?'

Let's reframe it as 'creative struggle'. When we help people through change, let's perform an act of grace. Let's hold the space in which creative struggle unfolds. You must accept that change unfurls. It's messy. It ebbs and flows, expands and contracts. It's the future, getting to know itself. Wriggling free from the fear of the unknown. Freeing itself from the primal fear: 'What if I'm not good enough?'[11]

This reminds me of when Artax, the hero Atreyu's horse, perishes in the 'Swamp of Sadness' in *The NeverEnding Story*. Thirty years on, I still have trust issues from this scene. Artax gives up and stops the creative struggle because he can't see his way through. That's where the change enabler roles come into play. A change manager is a change enabler. You are there to create the space in which permission and choice unfold. The unfolding of creative struggle. That's why you must bring a surety of purpose and unflagging vision of the future to your change recipients. You must keep the faith when others would backslide into hopelessness and overwhelm.

This, to me, is a better philosophy with which to understand the opposition to any change. Common sense keeps the individual safe. That's the function of any change reaction. The instinct for self-preservation makes it inevitable that there's some struggle.

Struggle is not resistance. Resistance implies a fixity of state. It also has adversarial and militaristic implications. It always makes me think of the Borg catch phrase, 'Resistance is futile.' The Borg method is also unfortunately how most change initiators react to any challenge to the future state. If we think of a change resister, then the tendency is to want 'to beat them into submission'. Or to 'win', which also really means 'beating them'. Now we're in them-and-us territory. This isn't conducive to change that sticks.

The notion of winners and losers is counter to successful change adoption. Change isn't a competition; it's a collaboration.

The competitive mindset is pretty common among those who seek out senior roles. These are your change initiators. It tends to come with the personality type that thrives in these positions. But when it comes to the change process, it can mean that some senior managers will default to 'winning the battle but losing the war'. If a you-will-do-this-OR-ELSE attitude is taken to leading people through change, then it becomes a pitched battle. All the energy of the change recipients goes into sabotaging the outcome. The dynamic of them-and-us between change initiators and change recipients brings out the worst in both. This flies in the face of the true meaning of 'leader-led change', when all must actually go together. Self-led change is a closer expression of what's really happening in a functional change adoption process.

If the project is a stupid idea, then people will resist. Good on them too. If it's a dumb change, then it's not change resistance: it's common sense.

But if the project is worthwhile, the reactivity is 'creative struggle'. The choice to change struggles against the fear and inertia that binds people to the current state. You, as the change manager, can't 'control the change'. But you can enable the conditions that move people closer to the opportunity to choose. The difference is that 'creative struggle' will move forward toward adoption, whereas resistance keeps things stuck.

There's a tool you can use to surface this creative struggle. Something to get your change initiators to listen and 'not bite down'. The tool is to hear the validity of the creative struggle. This tool I call 'the voice of the change'. I include this in all my change plans. It's also useful to prep for engagement briefings. And to help your learning team get ahead of what they might see in the learning sessions.

How creative struggle worked with FATCA

Let's look at the example of the 'Foreign Account Tax Compliance Act' (FATCA) project. A real 'project cat food' I refer to in chapter 4. This was the project in which new government legislation compelled all major banks in New Zealand to report their US-born customers. They also had to provide those people's Inland Revenue Service numbers to the US's tax department.

This is how the voice of change looked early in the project.

Staff say,

- This is way too much work.
- Our customers won't like it.
- X has been my customer for years. I'm not going to 'dob' them into the IRS.
- How do we reassure customers about their privacy?
- This is crazy! How am I supposed to ask good customers I've known for decades these questions? It's embarrassing and insulting to our loyal customers.

Customers say,

- This is why I left America.
- Why is my bank doing the IRS's dirty work?
- I already pay tax here.
- Why are you asking me?
- This is totally big brother behaviour.
- This is a complete invasion of privacy.
- It's none of your business.
- What's going to happen if I'm reported to the IRS?

Notice that these statements are 'keepin' it real'. They aren't glossing over the hard stuff. They are calling it out. They express what people will really think and feel about the coming change. Again, we're back to the essential function of the change manager to call out what is being avoided. You must name and own the elephants— large and small. They will trample all over your change adoption if you don't.

Let's look at what actions were used to address the voice of the change for the FATCA project.

Change Cat knew...

all the elephants had to be
diplomatically introduced.

Voice of the Change	Change Actions to Address
Bank Staff • This is way too much work. • Our customers won't like it. • X has been my customer for years. I'm not going to 'dob' them into the IRS. • How do we reassure customers about their privacy? • This is crazy! How am I supposed to ask good customers I've known for decades these questions? It's embarrassing and insulting to our loyal customers.	• Drive identification, review, reporting, and monitoring through system automation. • Move the due diligence to the back office. • Integrate the change to existing customer identification process rather than making it a separate process. • Communicate early and often— tell the story to bank staff of the obligation to comply.

	• Provide detailed scripting to manage the customer response. Provide collateral to re-direct to other 'first point of contacts' compliance sources like the National Banking Association.
Bank Customer • This is why I left America. • Why is my bank doing the IRS's dirty work? • I already pay tax here. • Why are you asking me? • This is totally big brother behaviour. • This is a complete invasion of privacy. • It's none of your business. • What's going to happen if I'm reported to the IRS?	• Advocate for industry-led communications through media and other external bodies. • Work closely with marketing to shape appropriate messages and intersperse with existing communications as a 'warm up'. • Use analytics to narrow down questioning of existing customers. Only ask those who are likely to meet criteria. • Seed standard messages across all customer channels to be used as required. • Make the story of why the bank has to comply front and centre in all comms. • Provide role-playing exercises for front-line staff. These give model answers for customer queries prior to launch.

How to gather the intel on the voice of the change

There was a lot of talk about the water cooler conversation in the 1990s. Still stands today, although it's unlikely to be around the water cooler. More likely while parking the bike downstairs, in the elevators, and when stacking the dishwasher together. Also, a quiet moment when leaving a meeting. Maybe on Microsoft Teams before everyone else joins or at the end. Sometimes at a work function.

To understand the voice of the change, let your spidey-senses tingle when you hear the truth talking. Again, if you're paying attention, you'll hear what you need to pursue in conversations.

Recently I worked on a large-scale change to the education sector. I got the best insights into the voice of the change from an outgoing employee. She had been with the organisation about nine years. For her, it was a 'what have I got to lose? I'm outta here' conversation. For me, that was gold.

If you're a consultant, you come into an environment and don't know where all the bodies are buried. You don't have years to develop a feel for the rhythms of the culture. You must quickly identify who is sensible. Who notices? Who gets both the overt and covert nuances of the environment? Who understands and cares about the project aspirations? Cultivate these people. Their insights are invaluable. They can translate the voice of the change for you. Their insights transform you from a clueless newbie. Now you're the person who is tight with the people who know where the bodies are buried.

Accept the offer, say 'yes' to the offer

In theatre sports, there's a key idea of 'Accept the offer.' The second idea is 'Always say yes to the offer.' In conversation, what that means is that you exercise the art of *quid pro quo*. You must give something to get something. You share an observation about possibility—not in a judgemental way, but in a curious way. You phrase it as an open-ended question.

Good open-ended questions to start the voice of the change conversation

Here are some examples of open-ended statements.

- 'I wonder if we might need … (a new person, a new function, a different perspective) … to help on that piece.'
- 'Do you feel our requirements are detailed enough to describe to vendors what we really need?'
- 'X seems a little distracted. I wonder what else is going on for them.'
- 'I was reflecting on whether we'd got to the heart of the issue we discussed in the meeting this morning.'

These statements might lead to a dead end or two. No harm done. Soon enough, you'll find someone who recognises and accepts the offer. That's if you stay in a state of receptivity. If you ask it in a neutral way. One that invites confidence. One that enables trust and confidence. One that isn't about judgement, but seeks to understand.

It also means that if someone makes an offer to give something, you accept it. This is within reason, of course. If you're reading the nonverbal cues in meetings, then you'll be able to tell who has more to say, but not in that meeting. Who didn't say anything, but certainly didn't agree with what was said?

The situation is always sending you 'the voice of change' message. Frequently, it is nonverbal. Often, it's unconscious. Just listen and watch.

It's there when people physically withdraw or shrink when more dominant voices speak. People's eyes slide away. Maybe their face gets fixed when someone expresses ideas they don't agree with. People come to the first session, but then stop showing up. People never show up and never respond to emails. These are the things to pay attention to. That's if you want to get to the heart of the change. The voice of the change is speaking to you. You shouldn't be satisfied until you've fully listened, then understood. Everything is talking to you—often more loudly than by using actual words. Where do the signs take you? Accept the offer.

This isn't intended to be a book about reading body language. But if this doesn't come to you like second nature, it's a skill worth cultivating. Culture doesn't only eat strategy for lunch, it'll eat your change adoption as well. Learn to love culture. Be acutely observant of people dynamics. People dynamics is a book all change managers need to read well.

Business change more often fails if the voice of the change isn't uncovered. There'll be no meaningful counters to the perceived downside of the change. When the project gets to delivery, all the unnamed elephants stampede. Stakeholders couldn't see their objections countered in the change support. Thoughts of achieving adoption get lost. Things degenerate to a reactive scramble just to save face and keep the wheels on.

If you master this, it's smooth sailing to high change adoption on delivery. That's because you've unwound the voice of change. You understood the essence of the change reaction. Then you developed valid responses on all issues.

On delivery, all the ripples and riptides will recede. You've smoothed the waters before they even had a chance to storm.

Summary

That's the end of chapter 7. This chapter covers how to understand the voice of change, then work out the counter measures to the adoption barriers. This rescues your change delivery BEFORE it's off the rails and it makes sure your change delivery sticks.

The core message of this chapter is that all change is a 'creative struggle'. It has an ebb and flow. The process of creative struggle reveals the 'voice of change'. That's the ebb of the 'pull' back to the current state. The ebb reveals what's hardest about your change to get adopted. Thoughts and feelings, no matter how incoherent, must be surfaced and understood. Only named elephants can be addressed. The creative struggle must be known, recognised, validated, and mitigated. Seat the elephants at your table. They are not 'enemies' to be vanquished. They are signs pointing the way to make the change stick.

In the next chapter, we'll look at how to deal with project resets and reframes.

CHAPTER 8

Reframes and Resets

On any business change journey, there are always forks in the road and the occasional loop track. What matters most is how you deal with them and how you're seen to deal with them.

How to rock the crunchy stuff

This chapter, boiled right down, is super simple: Be authentic in how you deal with your bad news and 'get ugly early'. This is a pointed way of saying, 'If you have something not so great to say, don't fudge it and don't delay it.' Get it out as soon as possible and then move on to how you're going to fix it, in the same communication.

Not all news is good news in business project land. That's inevitable. What you want everyone to remember is how you owned it, how decisive you were about owning it, and how you rose above the crunchy stuff.

Two projects

Let's tell a cautionary tale of two projects.

Project one is the product development and launch of a new credit card. It replaces an existing credit card product. A long-term, much loved one. It offers a cool reward points system through partnership with another organisation's service. Unfortunately, the account with that business partner is lost. Dark rumours have been circulating about the account, and how it's been in jeopardy for almost a year. The account manager who managed the relationship with that commercial partner went to a competitor bank some months ago. Teams from marketing and sales to back-office credit card fulfilment know something's up. An alternative credit card product is hastily scratched together. However, the lost business partnership means the 'jewel in the crown' rewards scheme is gone.

On launch day of the new credit card product, an internal article unfurls at the top of the intranet. 'Time for something new', brags the headline. The first sentence leads with, 'We've enjoyed a long relationship, but now it's time for something new.' The problem is everyone in the organisation knows it's a lie. If the business relationship with the partner could have been salvaged, it would have been. There'd be no inferior new product. We didn't have something new because we wanted to. We had something 'new' because we lost the good thing we had. And we were desperate to save face. The business partner relationship was lost because it wasn't managed well so the business partner got annoyed and decided to do business elsewhere. Simple. Why would the organisation give up one of the most successful products it ever launched?

That was the one time, in that organisation, that I saw an incredibly loyal employee base falter. They blinked in disbelief and said some exasperated and pretty cynical things. Trust was betrayed in a major way.

The lesson is this—never fly in the face of the bleeding obvious. Be straight up in your communications. Don't play your audience for a fool. It won't wash and it's disrespectful.

Deflective spin doctoring never lands well. It lacks authenticity. Your culture has already sniffed out the truth. Culture is testing you to see if you're prepared to admit the mistake and then show you're big enough and capable enough to come up with a workable solution. Culture never sleeps, and its gaze is indeed pitiless in moments of crisis.[12]

The change manager must be tenacious in a fight in these situations. Usually with your own senior stakeholders. Remember chapter 2 and what senior stakeholders want to move toward? Being the bearer of bad news is not high on their list of favourite things to do, or really on anyone's, for that matter. In these situations, it's the role of the change manager to broker the value of authenticity. You need to anticipate and spell out the blow-back from inauthentic messages. Paint a clear picture of the downstream consequences of trying to 'skew the pitch'. Sell the value of facing into, not away from, bad news.

There's also a cumulative consequence to the avoidance of unpleasant, but necessary, news. If you keep spin doctoring the curly things, your change recipients will lose faith. They get change fatigue. Or is it 'inauthenticity fatigue'? Eventually, they'll succumb to numb indifference. Numb indifference and high adoption do not jam at the same joints.

How to communicate 'bad' news

Here is an example of a reset communication for project delivery delay:

Greeting,

The delivery date for xxxx has been reset to xxxx. This is because xxxx [enter the factors that have caused the reset— be clear and succinct, don't labour the point]. Planning is being undertaken to ensure all learning, pilot, and so on is aligned to the new date.

Here is something good about the opportunity the revised date brings. This is where you can go for more information. I'll be coming back to confirm next steps on [such and such a date].

[Sign off]

Here are the key points to note on the example above:

1. Get to the point quickly.

2. Don't pad out your message with statements about how hard working the team is or how hard the team and the leaders tried to avoid whatever happened.

3. Put the key point in the first or second sentence. People seldom read beyond the first two sentences of a mass communication email.

4. State clearly what is being done to ensure the reset is a success.

5. Acknowledge specifically how any requirements of change recipients will be adjusted to accommodate the reset. Have the learning dates changed? Will more on-the-ground support be in place on go-live? Will the pilot be extended?

6. Be clear about the next follow-up communication, and when and what it will cover.

7. Make sure you do communicate next steps on the exact date you said you would.

Expectation Management

A note on expectation management at the start of projects. When you start, the less surety you have. For a period, your change recipients will grant you grace. You can be a little unspecific about what exactly is happening and when. At this stage, you can get away with phrases in engagement like these:

- 'We expect ...'
- 'It is anticipated that ...'
- 'Once xxxx happens we will confirm ...'
- 'There is an opportunity to do xxxx'
- 'It is likely that ...'

However, I would watch the overuse of the word 'potential'. This could be a pet peeve. I've worked on projects where 'potential' was a major eye-roll word. One project required the setup of a small back-office risk management team. For the first year, it was insisted that the team described this new function as 'potential'. Privately, the team wondered if the organisation had a secret stash of Oompa Loompas. Would these be magicked up to fulfil the very real and not at all 'potential' processing requirements at the appointed hour? Because, if we didn't have a secret stash of Oompa Loompas, we really needed to get a move on and recruit this team. In fact, it was a key requirement. The REAL (not potential) members of this team needed workspace, a reporting line, and food and rations pronto.

So, let's not downplay non-negotiable deliverables just because they'll be unpopular. This causes increased angst at go-live. The 'kick the can down the road' game has to end. Best to be proactive and definitely preferable to everyone running round in a reactive panic at go-live.

In the new required team example above, the use of the word 'potential' had consequences. It took a year and a half to land agreement that this new team was needed. There's only so much road (map) to kick these cans down. Then hard talks will happen when tempers run high. Often for less favourable outcomes. Better to deal with it earlier when cooler heads prevail.

A side bar on the 'potential' story above. Projects, and particularly large-scale programmes, often get locked into their own rhetoric. As the custodians of authentic speak, the change manager must rise above this. It's a hard corner to stand in, against deflective and avoidant messaging, but a necessary one. Politicians practise the art of deflection, but change managers should not. It doesn't mean there isn't an appropriate time, place, medium, and tone to the message, but it's not to be avoided.

'Get ugly early' as a strategy isn't only for communications. It applies to your whole project execution. Sitting on unavoidable bad news, once you know the bad news is inexorable, only ever doubles

Change Cat knew...
when it comes to project snags, snarls, and
hairballs...

it's best to get ugly early!

the pain when you finally get to it. You can't get to the good news on the other side of something ugly until you've owned the something and named it.

The name of the game is always anticipation. Have your ear to the ground. Take the pulse of the organisation. That's from the board and executive to the cleaning staff. From executive assistants and all types of advisors to random people you chat with in the kitchen. These are often the most valuable sources of intel you have.

The constant flow of intel is the key reason why your change impact assessment is a living document. Refresh this every two months to keep the WIIFMs juicy and current.

Once learning invitations are sent, this is the point of no return for generalist messages. From now on, language must be specific, not general. This is a huge watershed moment. You're at the point where, for the end user, 'sh!t just got real'. No user or manager of a team of users will settle for 'we expect', 'it is anticipated', 'we hope', at this stage. That language would 'spook the horse'.

When the change is imminent, the environment is thirsty for certainty. All communication and engagement must now deliver clarity and surety. Learning invitation release means all change recipients have only one question. That question is, 'What do I do on day one?' That's on a step-by-step basis. From this point, everything must clearly signpost the road to certainty and no surprises.

The usual types of resets and reframes

For change projects, here's a list of the usual types of resets and reframes you should expect to see. Anticipate them and watch for early signs of them.

- Software-dependent delays.
- Infrastructure-dependent delays.

- Delays to reading of legislation and passing into law.

- If infrastructure is involved, hardware complications.

- If integration is involved, issues on functional testing.

- If software and/or hardware is involved, there is no dedicated test environment, inadequate end-to-end testing, and user acceptance testing.

- Penetration testing reveals issues with infrastructure.

- There was no pilot trial and now the first change recipients are in mutiny.

- Inadequate time for development and delivery of learning. The absolute minimum tight development timeframe is four months, whether through e-learning or classroom-based learning.

- If learning is part of the scope, then the appropriate activities and mechanisms to ensure successful learning delivery have been missed. This could be that there is no project pilot, no learning IT environment set up, no quality and comprehensive learning data (must be anonymised) set up for learners to use during training, and no established learning data refresh process or learning data owner to run the data refresh. This means that the learning system gets cluttered up with the data entered by the previous learners during the learning exercises.

- Delivery of go-live has no IT support, no system administrator, no vendor access.

- Change of sponsor and/or project manager and/or executive sponsor.

- Loss of access to crucial subject matter expertise.

- Change of vendor.

- Loss of budget.

- Significant re-scope or project team restructure.

The good news is that everything usually has a reframe and/or reset of some kind. You need to expect it, plan for it, and make it part of life's rich tapestry. Face into it and you can get on with the good news about what's beyond it.

The old adage in customer service is even more applicable in change management: 'A happy customer tells four to five people. But an unhappy customer who has their problem fixed tells six people.' That unhappy customer becomes more brand loyal than the customers who had a good experience in the first place![13]

Change management is a lot about making deposits at the bank of human trust and confidence. The sooner you own the bad news and turn it toward the good, the bigger the bank balance will get. You would be surprised how many withdrawals you can make from this bank. But only if there's been consistent proactive, honest, and authentic communication. Get ugly early when you must, then point forward to the North Star beyond.

Managing politics and ego

There's always plenty of politics and egos on business change projects. Selling to senior executives that it's better to 'get ugly early' can be tough. But a fundamental role of the change manager is to be the anticipator of unintended consequence.

Good language to position these conversations would start with

- 'I wonder what would happen if we …?'
- 'Are we sure we're comfortable that …?'
- 'How could it look if we …?'
- 'What could we be missing here?'

Wondering about alternate possibilities is a great 'safe' way to introduce alternative approaches in a less adversarial manner. You also want to gather your evidence. There is nothing so valuable as seeding a crucial conversation with effective influencers in the room, influencers who are already primed to reinforce the desired outcome. By the time you get into most important meetings, the outcome needs to be a fait accompli. It's the meetings before the meeting that count on the big-ticket items.

Be savvy about how and when and who delivers the 'not so good news'. I've worked on many projects, pumping the agenda of 'leader-led change'. All the leaders trumpeting the message were leaders no one wanted to follow. This happens a lot. This is when the organisation's informal network of influencers comes to the fore. Here, you play a 'shell game'. Arm these leaders with appropriate scripts. Then let these leaders front the webinars and the team sessions and the executive briefings. They'll be happy and feel 'in control'.

Meanwhile, back at the ranch, you've recruited your army of influencers. These are the people on the ground who the change recipients actually respect. Identify them, cultivate them, and use them well. They tell the story of the change, the gains made, and the pain avoided. Use them to articulate the bad news. Then they reinforce again the story of the gain the change brings.

It's showbiz—End on a high note

Finally, I hope it's come through in this chapter that you must be upfront with the bad news, but always end on a high note. Communication and engagement must be done in an authentic way. Don't try and claim high ground you can't legitimately own. But, say for instance your bad news is about a delivery delay or a reduction in scope. These are both very common. There's room here to expand on the opportunity the extra time brings. The scope reduction is tougher. Still, if what was promised proved impossible to deliver, then it's better to get something than nothing at all. This one is often saved by selling a phased delivery approach. One with plenty of time for test and learn. There are always options. Test hard messages with a few key change recipients. Always have some in the project tent. This keeps things honest. Use them as a litmus test for the crunchiest news.

Finally, remember that change management has aspects of performance sport. All the world's a stage (of perceptions). Leave them wanting more. For business change management, that means always end by pointing to the aspiration. What are you working to achieve? Reaffirm why it's worth taking the journey.

Summary

That's the end of chapter 8. Now that you've finished this chapter, you understand why and how to own the bad news. First rule, be upfront. Do it quickly, clearly, and crisply. Don't make excuses. Finish by talking about the good stuff on the other side of the bad news.

The core message of this chapter is that it never pays to delay or deflect significant bad news. Senior stakeholders and large projects generally tend to want to avoid the bad news. But it's the opposite that earns all the brownie points for trust and confidence. Authenticity is the coin of the realm for change management that sticks. Of course, there's a right time and place for everything. But there's no substitute for clear messaging. Messages that 'own the ugly' and then move briskly on to opportunity. Your change recipients will watch closely. Then they'll lean in a little closer IF YOU'RE AUTHENTIC. They want to warm themselves. Be warmed by a spark of genuine human connection. A warmth based on courage, honesty, and respect for the people the change would serve.

In the next chapter, we'll look at how to set up for successful adoption via your change-readiness activity.

·

CHAPTER 9

Change Readiness and Success Measurement

Back in the day, change readiness was not such a formal thing. You did it, but it was more of a seat-of-the-pants thing that you got a feel for as you went. A lot of the time you just talked to people.

In the early 2000s, this moved more toward formal surveys delivered via email links to a survey portal. That's tricky these days. There's so much change fatigue. Let's face it, just general fatigue and overwhelm. This means the pendulum has swung back a bit from intensive electronic surveying. You need to think about this before you decide how to approach your readiness activity.

Making change matter

My recommendation is that you always supplement any electronic surveying with something else. Focus groups are essential. There are many funky apps to make these fun and less painful experiences. The odd digital poll or collective word cloud never goes amiss either. I'll list some good ones in the notes section at the end of this book.[14]

Whatever combination of mediums you use, have a broad cross-section in the sample. Ones that represent all levels in the organisational hierarchy and your key external groups.

Three phases of readiness

Readiness typically has three phases. The purpose of each phase is as follows.

1. Readiness baseline—survey one. This covers 'What do the change recipients think and feel about the change?' That's BEFORE there's a detailed picture of what the change looks like in the future state. The result report from this survey establishes your baseline.

2. Readiness pre-go-live check—survey two. This covers 'What do people think and feel about the change just prior to it happening?' This is done on the eve of doing the new thing. That is when change recipients have a detailed picture of what lies ahead, but they haven't experienced it in real time yet.

3. Readiness post-go-live (success measurement)—survey three. This covers 'How did it go? Were the outcomes achieved? How much adoption to date? What remains? What are the barriers? What are the metrics that prove benefit realisation has been achieved?' These are measures of the change management's success.

Readiness has become quite complex over the last decade. I've seen some remarkably giant spreadsheets used to manage it. I'm not a fan. No matter how giant your project or programme is.

The fundamentals remain, at heart, simple. Your people (recipients) will be ready when you have the following covered.

- What is changing?
- Why is it changing?

- What's the good that will come out of the change (for each impacted individual)?
- How is it changing (what will they do differently)?
- When is it changing?
- What are the incentives to make the change?
- What are the disincentives to make the change?
- How are change recipients supported to make the change?
- Where do people go for help?

Your readiness approach shouldn't be hard. If you make it hard, you make the change look hard. It should look easy. Something that invites participation.

Make sure you get your survey audience right. You want to survey only those about to move through a significant change in state. If they're only bystanders to the change, don't survey them. If respondents aren't directly impacted, they have no skin in the game. They won't be motivated to complete the survey. If they do complete it, it's likely they'll skew your results to the point there's no value in them. It's very hard to report anything meaningful up the food chain from middle-of-the-road survey results. For example, '73 percent of respondents are neutral about the change. Neither excited, nor unexcited.' Hard to plan your next change intervention off that!

Four-point scale: How excited are you about the change?

Here's a tip on your survey assessment scale. To avoid middle-of-the-road survey results, you want to assess each question on a four-point and NOT a five-point scale. Here's an example:

1. Not excited at all.
2. A little bit excited.

3. Quite excited.

4. Very excited.

If you use this scale, then you force your respondents to choose either 'more in' or 'more out'. This gives a clearer collective result to work with. It removes the option for respondents to fence sit on a 'three'. Which is about as useful as no answer at all. If you give them the option, a reasonable proportion of your respondents will opt for the middle ground response. So don't offer it. It's never fun to report up to the leadership team that 'most respondents are in the "meh" space about the change'. You want people to choose whether they are overall supportive or not.

I was once brought on to a large programme after they'd done the first readiness survey. A pilot group of thirty people was about to go through a significant change of state. However, one-thousand-plus dutiful operations staff had been surveyed. No surprises that the survey result was the ultimate 'meh'. People were unsure if they could really describe what the change was. People were unclear how ready they were to make the change (that they didn't understand and weren't close to anyway). People were unclear on whether they needed to know more about the change or when they needed to know it.

It's hard to work with 'meh'. Better to get an early result in your first survey that indicates a strong opposition to the change, to get clear reasons why the change isn't desirable and won't achieve what it sets out to do. This you can get a grip on. The 'meh' response, not so much. It's too inconclusive to give any clear picture of what to do to address the obstacles.

Here we're back to the notion of change resistance, or better, 'change reaction'. The change reaction will be directly proportionate to how great, or how silly, the original change idea is. Readiness surveys will soon tell you how much value the change is perceived to deliver. And that's key, right there. Perception is nine-tenths of reality. A change that delivers loads of value counts for nothing if it's not perceived to deliver that value.

Loads of HR research proves that people want to do good work. Most of all, people want to feel that what they do adds value.[15] That's the emotional connection to the work. When they feel that what they do really matters. People also generally want their organisation to succeed. Be better, faster, more efficient, more effective, more profitable, more competitive, and provide more quality. All reflected in wages, benefits, and development opportunities, of course. More of all the right stuff.

But people will oppose your not-so-great change idea. In these cases, it's not resistance, it's change reaction to a lack of common sense.

Survey one questions for baseline readiness

- How much do you know about the change?
- How clear are you about what the change is?
- How clear are you about what the change will mean for you?
- Do you have an idea of how the change will impact you?
- Are you clear on why the change is happening?
- Have you seen any communications about what's changing?
- How relevant to you are the communications you've seen?
- Has your people leader spoken to you about the changes?
- How concerned are you about your ability to make the change?
- Do you know where to go to learn more about the change?

Survey one—Good free text questions for baseline readiness

- What's most on your mind about the change?
- What are you most excited about with the coming change?
- Do you think the change is needed? If not, why not?
- What would be more valuable?

My guide for surveys is no more than eight questions. This includes the free text questions. Don't make your survey or your questions hard, long, or onerous. Everything you do is a calling card for the coming change. Culture is watching. If you make the readiness survey—or any other of your change interventions—long, hard, boring, and onerous, then, guess what people read about the coming change.

The delivery channels, structure, tone, and content of your change activities matter. No one's going to want to do it if you make it look hard. Complex materials and exercises are inaccessible. For great engagement, make it easy and inviting. If you remember nothing else from this book, remember this: it is your job to make the complex simple. There is no virtue in making stuff hard. Complex and hard are the enemies of high adoption. People use what works, what's simple, and what's convenient. Massive bonus points if you make it fun.

On this note, the bigger the project, the more it tends to put everything through the 'complicater'. Doing big pieces IS complex. But you won't make the change stick if you follow the trend and keep things complex in the change space. If other project roles are the complicaters, the change manager is 'The Simplifier'. You balance out all the other complicated people and stuff required to get it done. Wear your 'Simplifier' badge with pride. It is you the change recipients will look to when things get real just before go-live.

You also need to defend the space when there's pressure to complicate. Early on, senior stakeholders can put on a lot of pressure. They need the project to be seen to be doing stuff. It makes them feel good about themselves and looks good to their peers and boss. These groups are used to looking at large and complex documents. Therefore, there's an assumption that this is required and necessary. Better to keep it simple and build genuine understanding. Otherwise, nobody gets it.

Plenty of your senior stakeholders won't get it either—it's just that they'll never say that. At least not to you.

Really big programmes of work can turn into a giant consultant p!ssing contest. The mentality nose dives into 'My methodology is better than yours.' Or 'My methodology brings all the users to the yard.' This happens when the programme drinks too much of its own Kool-Aid. You get the smiley Smurf stamp for holding the line.

Instead keep it simple and intelligible, and deliver it in bite-sized, easily digestible chunks. Ones that everyone can swallow. You aren't there to compete with the other consultants. You're there to achieve high change adoption.

The baseline readiness survey is one of the first things you will do on a large scale. It's change's first major calling card with the change recipients. Use it to show your key point of difference from everyone else on the project. You want your audience to get a feel for you from the way you transact with them. Survey and focus group participants should leave feeling, 'I can trust this change manager. They were straight and they talked our language. They'll see me right and help me understand all this.'

You need to be the guide to clarity and certainty.

A few years ago, I worked on a large-scale transformation programme. An external team came in to run a session to look at how we tackled an upcoming change activity. No materials were circulated prior to the meeting. The discussion document was a giant series of A3 excel spreadsheets in eight-point font. This was stuck on a white board that we sat around in a breakout space. Some of us were at least four metres from the board.

The session started with the facilitators asking us, 'What do you think of the spreadsheet?'

I KID YOU NOT!

This is the kind of behaviour that would make a change manager weep. Nobody can read a giant, super complex spreadsheet in eight-point font. Nobody can process that giant data vivisection and make sense of it in a session. Or probably ever. This is anti-change management. Operating like this as a change manager means you've lost your way.

So, keep it simple. A research-backed rule of thumb is that at any one time people can remember seven, plus or minus two, pieces of information.[16] In complex environments, when people already have a super full-on day, I reckon it's more like five pieces, max. Keep that in mind for all the change collateral you develop. This means you chunk up the learning into key concepts. These roll up into sets of information with about five key components. You write articles and leader-led scripts with no more than five, and preferably three, key points. If it's a PowerPoint, definitely no more than three key points per slide. Even better, go with a picture and one or two sentences a slide.

Sophisticated thinking isn't complicated thinking. The thinking behind it might be complex. The manner of expression is simple. That's true sophistication for a business change manager. You are a sense maker.

If you don't observe these rules, people will think you're crazy and switch off, or lose interest. Specificity of language matters. If you're using simple words, and fewer of them, you have to use the right ones. If a survey is for a thousand people, then write a simple survey. Then you could get a 50 percent response rate of five hundred people. That's better than a complex survey with a 5 percent response rate of fifty people.

Be absolutely clear on who your survey audience is. There's often a tension here. You're surveying your change recipients. But approval comes from the leadership team on the project. Change initiators in leadership teams are VERY different from change recipients. The leadership team may be impressed and accustomed to long and complex documents. Their assumption will be that business readiness assessments are the same. They're not.

Remember, you are the custodian of high change adoption. Be clear and explicit with your leaders why a simple, user-friendly approach works. Outline the road to make the change stick. Complexity is a detour into confusion and low buy-in. Again, use your advisory change recipients to help make the case. I've noticed that operations staff from the coalface have much more influence on the decisions of senior operational managers. This generally holds true for all functions.

To increase the survey response rate, it can be very helpful to offer incentives. These don't have to be large; they just have to hit the right mark.

On a survey I ran in the banking sector across 3,743 change recipients, we ran a draw with four chances at a prize if the survey was completed by a certain date. All respondents by the set date went into a draw for four chances at 250 shopping points. These could be used to buy goods or services. The overall cost to the organisation to offer this was very minimal. The uptake rate was one of the highest I've ever achieved, hitting over the 80 percent response rate.

Anything above a 60 percent response rate is pretty good. That's being realistic. Change initiators will often have a highly over-inflated idea of how many respondents you'll get. Make sure the expectations are aligned before you report the readiness result. If not, the change initiators will focus on how poor they think the overall response rate is, rather than on how rich the findings are. This can invalidate your readiness efforts before they've got very far out of the starting gate.

Write succinct launch emails for all your change activities. The average worker receives 140 emails per day.[17] As people eyeball their inbox, yours is already in the 'low priority' tray. It's not from the boss asking where an urgent late piece of work is! Get to the point quickly. State clearly in the title what the activity is and why it's worth doing.

The body of the email must be less than the recipient's screen size. People never scroll down for these types of emails. What you want them to do, by when, and why must be stated clearly in the first couple of sentences.

Remember people rarely read beyond the second sentence. It's useful to break these emails up into chunks with clear bold headings. 'Your Action' with a statement like, 'Click on this link to complete a short survey and go in the draw to win xxxx' works well.

When you get to your pre-go-live readiness survey, this is the real showtime for change management. Design a survey focus group to check that people are ready to make the change. The survey invites people to verify their readiness and willingness to move into the future state. You are at the point when the gap between the current and future state needs to be very, very small. People must be in a high state of readiness to make the change stick. Learning is done and any final mop-up sessions are in progress. The go-live support team is prepped and the daily go-live triage model is in place and raring to go. Superusers and change champions have done their influencing work and are standing by. Your change recipients should now be more focussed on the future-state horizon just ahead than on the 'old' current state.

Survey two—Pre-go-live questions

Here's a list of good questions for the pre-go-live survey (survey two):

- How ready are you to make the change?
- How confident are you about your ability to make the change?
- How much do you agree with the reasons why the change is happening?
- How competent do you feel to make the change?
- How clear are you about where to go for support?
- How excited are you about the change?

Good free text questions for the pre-go-live survey:

- What are you most excited about?
- What are you hearing about the project?
- Do you feel anything has been missed?
- Is there anything you're not confident about? Why?

Survey three—Post-go-live success measurement

In my experience, this one honestly doesn't get done that often. There are heaps of promises and detailed PowerPoints near the start about how it will be done. But post-go-live, enthusiasm dwindles. So does the number of people on the project team! Often, your senior sponsors have shifted their focus some time ago. If you got the change live and it went okay, you're already less of a problem child than many others. Humans have short attention spans for project follow through. Change initiators always have other fires to fight and mountains to climb. This is why it's so hard to build a quantum of evidence that the change activities actually helped. So, it is doubly important to get this one done, because this is how you build change management into an organisation as an enduring continuous improvement cycle. One that gets runs on the board and grows organisational maturity. That's only when the value of change is measured and understood. Then the learnings can be fed back into the next change.

The trick here is to ensure you don't just measure what's implemented but rather what's adopted and by how much.

If you only measure how many widgets were delivered, you are back to the 'so what?' factor of chapter 3. Here's a list of these types of implementation measures that are good as far as they go, but they don't measure outcomes:

- How many people enrolled in learning?
- How many people went to learning?
- How many people passed learning?
- How many people attended briefings?
- How many people attended webinars?
- How many hits on a web page?
- Duration of stay on web page?
- Number of downloads of attachments?

This is widget measurement that tells you nothing about whether outcomes are achieved.

These types of measures are okay, particularly at the start of the project. They get a bit of momentum going to show that some engagement is happening. At least in terms of volumes and frequency of encounters. Senior stakeholders love some good, meaty stats on engagement. Particularly when projects are just out of the starting gate and need 'runs on the board'.

But effective measurement of adoption are outcomes-related measures. The key focus of the measure is to discern, 'How much is the change being used? Has performance improved since the change went in?'

Here's a list of these outcomes adoption measures:

- More?
- Faster?
- More efficient?
- Better quality?
- More user-friendly?
- Higher volume?
- Less cost?
- More profit?
- More uptake?
- More customer loyalty?
- More new customers?
- More market share?

This is when old school measures like the business balanced score card can be useful.[18] You want to tie the success measurement outcomes back to the whole organisational strategy. What has the change contributed to targets for process improvement, performance management, finances, engagement, and service satisfaction?

Your success measurement surveying should ask things like this:

- How much are you using the change? If you're not using it, why is that?
- What are the obstacles?
- How do you assess your level of confidence using the change?
- How do you measure your competence?
- What would help you to be more competent?
- What would help you to be more confident?
- What follow-up support do you need?

If you want to do this measurement in a way that's truly meaningful, you can't have it flapping in the breeze. Connect it to the organisational strategic measures. Get some hard metrics. Anything that shows improvement to mission purpose and/or bottom line will be hugely valuable. Of course, this depends on the size of what you're delivering. But if it's anything relating to increased efficiency, quality, or increased return (monetary or other), then these are immensely valuable measures to have.

You need a through-line that tells the story from baseline readiness survey one to post-go-live success measurement survey three. Then you want to relate the measures from survey three to the wider organisational context.

The strongest relational measure achieved out of a project I've worked on was this: 'A 45 percent reduction in calls to the HR Help Line in the first four weeks post the new HR KnowledgeBase go-live.'

Summary

That's the end of chapter 9. Now you have an outline of the three-phased approach to successful change readiness and examples of what to include in each survey. You understand how to write an effective survey launch email. Also, you understand the value of incentives to increase the response rate. Most important, you understand the difference between implementation measures and outcome adoption measures. The statistics on delivered widgets are second fiddle to the uptake measures.

This chapter also talks about the importance of linking your business readiness results to the wider organisational performance management and strategic measures.

The core message of this chapter is that change readiness matters, but keep it simple. The way you survey is very important. Gear it to attract the change recipients to the change. For your success measurement, don't just measure widgets. This tells you nothing about how much the change has been adopted or the value derived from the adoption. Always supplement large scale surveying with focus groups. This provides context. Dialogue gives the richest insight into the change reaction and what to do about it.

In chapter 10, our next and final chapter, we'll look at how to transition the delivered change to permanent business owners.

CHAPTER 10

Making the Change Stick

I could have called this chapter, 'Hot Potato, Hot Potato', because business ownership is often a hot potato. It's not easy to get business ownership of a new thing welcomed with open arms. I've seen many rounds of 'chuck the hot potato' with many implemented changes. Initially, most stakeholders are desperate not to be left holding the hot potato when the music stops!

How to enable successful business handover

To understand this, it's back to our chapter 2 key point that people want to move toward gain and away from pain. Business ownership is no different. At first, business ownership of a new thing often looks like 'more stuff to do with the same money and people'. It's not an easy win. That's until you sell it. Selling is an integral part of change management. Not in the shiny suit, used car salesman sense of the word. But in the digging out the true nuggets of change sense, to celebrate everyday sense.

Change Cat knew securing your business owner...
was like passing a hot potato!

First rule of business ownership is to pinpoint who is compelled to care about the delivered change outcome. Who already has accountability for the outcomes the change contributes to? Who cares most about the value delivered long after the project team is gone?

The potential business owners who are happy to take on new stuff at the first whiff tend to be the empire builders. If you read that a 'land grab' is motivating the willingness, then you had better look harder. A manager's desire to acquire more staff and budget is not a great reason to give them ownership. These stakeholders will take on anything, but they aren't necessarily your ideal business owner. Often quite the reverse.

I've witnessed several projects flounder at the last possible moment. Often when many things were done well. That's often because the motivations of the successful business owner weren't well understood. They didn't align with genuine commitment to ongoing sustainability of the delivered change value.

Be mindful that there are two distinct types of ongoing business ownership. The two types of business ownership are these.

1. Business ownership of the delivered outputs of the projects. Tactical business ownership includes, for example, the software and hardware installed, the processes and policies handed over.

2. Business ownership of the outcomes and benefits of what's delivered. The realised change value. This is the ownership of the sustained change value the project delivers. For example, the change increased customer satisfaction, decreased time to production, or increased profit.

These are two completely different things. They need different business owners. It's important not to get confused between them.

Further, keep in mind that the mechanics of, say, the policy change, are achieved when the new policy is launched. But the change is only successful when the users adopt the new policy. This is measured by the realisation of long-term benefits. *Outcome* is the tangible result delivered. *Benefit* is the measurable improvement delivered by the outcome.

What needs ownership

First of all, you need to be clear about what needs ownership. At the tactical level, that's usually some, or all, of the following.

- Continuous improvement process.
- IT support model.
- Learning deliverables—lesson plans, quick reference guides, e-learning modules, learner guides and workbooks, facilitator guides.

- New and/or revised key performance indicators.

- New induction materials.

- New or amended channels.

- New or amended internal and/or external marketing collateral.

- New or amended policy.

- New or amended process.

- New or amended products or services.

- New or enhanced or upgraded IT software and/or hardware.

- New organisational design functions or teams or roles within teams.

- Ongoing measurements.

- Performance management changes or additions.

- Performance measures.

- Standard operating procedures and their associated business rules.

You can identify your business owners through your governance structure. Often some or all of your key business owners will be within your steering committee or board. Look for them in whatever forum you use to bring together your project decision-makers.

On a side note, if you look around that forum and don't see the true owners of the delivered outcome, that's an issue. Often these forums are set up long before the change manager arrives on the scene. The bullet list above relates to the tactical 'widget' level of what's delivered. If when you arrive on the scene you realise that only widget owners have been identified and not realised outcome owners, then you need to intervene. Be clear with your change initiators about what you need ownership of. Cover why and what the accountability of this enduring ownership means.

Start the conversation on business ownership as soon as possible. Once you're out of your analysis and design phases, it's time to prime the pump on business ownership. Statements in your steering committee pack seeking ownership need to really spell it out. Here are some examples of statements to use when seeking business ownership.

- The project requires ownership of xxxx by xxxx date.
- The ownership will entail xxxx (what the owner will have to do, how often, when).
- This ownership is required because (enter the reasons why).
- The ownership is accountable to track the following metrics xxxx. This is to measure the sustained realisation of the change value.
- The review cycle recommendation for the ownership xxxx for xxxx reasons.
- The resource and cost implications of this ownership are anticipated to be xxxx operating expenses and xxxx capital expenses annually.

The opportunities business ownership will bring are xxxx. State what the advantages of the ownership are.

Develop strong WIIFMs for your business ownership. It will be things like these.

- More control and early awareness of events so that they can be proactively managed.
- Early opportunity to anticipate certain market advantages and disadvantages.
- Early sightline to development and delivery issues.
- Early sightline to customers or staff engagement.
- Insight into growing capability gaps.

You may need to seek ownership of new staff (a group, or function, or additional roles in an existing team). If so, tell the story of how these people will fit into and enable the whole.

Here are some key questions for new team ownership conversations.

- How do the new staff fit into the end-to-end business model and what is the value they bring?

- Are they a risk and assurance function that will act as a 'canary in the coal mine' providing early detection of upcoming issues?

- Do they have a creative function that will shine a light on continuous improvement or innovation opportunities?

- Do they do something else?

We're back to the fundamental need to be explicit about the value brought. THEN sell that value in the WIIFM statements. Business owners are key change recipients even though they're usually also change initiators. Help your prospective business owner to feel good about having more hungry mouths to feed.

Often the organisation will already be in some kind of restructure as you seek these owners. Make sure you stay across any organisational changes to roles and reporting lines. There are usually winners and losers out of all restructures. Your new business owners need to be winners in the future state, not displaced from the current state. It's a major bummer to get a win and finally identify a willing business owner, then realise their role is going in four to six months!

Owners of the delivered change value for a new system

Let's look at a specific project delivery example to understand the difference between the tactical and delivered value for business owners.

Say the project delivers an IT system. Information technology and digital have ownership of the system delivery, maintenance, and enhancement. But the owner of the change value depends on what the system enables.

- Customer relationship management system delivers value for sales and marketing.
- Enterprise documentation and records management system delivers value for an information management function or, if you're lucky, even a knowledge management function (although those seem to have gone out of favour since the 1990s!). Often in my experience these end up being owned by Finance. Yikes! Putting this ownership with the bean counters is not usually great for achieving creative and innovate curation of the organisation's information, knowledge, and wisdom assets for maximum business advantage.
- Human resource information system delivers value to the human resources function.

Ask yourself the following question to get a bead on who your likely realised value business owners are. 'Who cares most if this fails?'

The answer to this question is the function that has the most skin in the game. The people carrying out this function value the realisation of the benefits the most. And they feel the pain of the consequence if the value isn't realised the most. Therefore, they're the likely custodians of the delivered change value.

Sometimes the owner of the realised change value is less obvious. Going back to the 'outcomes onion' will help clarify who that owner is. Who lies at the heart of outcome? Will the REAL outcome business owner please stand up!

The owner of the sustained change value was less obvious

In one company that hired me, the strategic policy team designed a new policy to improve how requests for funding would be developed and assessed. The strategic development team built the artefacts to implement the policy. The investment partner teams in operations worked with the external change recipients. They help them adapt to the new funding approach. The investment funding teams in operations assessed and approved or declined the funding bids. The planning and construction teams in operations worked with the regional bodies to build the funded assets. The support services finance team oversaw the funding. The chief financial officer (CFO) had the ultimate accountability to stay within the overall funding envelopment.

In this case, the CFO was the project's senior responsible officer. However, if you asked yourself, 'Who's closest to the coalface? Who lives the dream when the change goes live?' you would come up with a different answer. It would be the operations teams who work with the local councils to develop the funding bids and then construct the funded assets. In this case, I would argue, operations have a much stronger stake in the business ownership of the delivered value. They are the ones who will get it in the neck from the change recipients if the assets aren't built.

Business ownership of regulatory deliverables

Business ownership for regulatory change pieces is even harder. These are traditionally known as 'project cat food'. You must have them in the fridge—but they're a bit smelly, and no one likes having them around. It's very hard to get ongoing ownership of project cat foods. It's even more important to start the process of finding the business owners early. Usually, the value delivered from these pieces is as follows.

1. Get audit and regulatory approval and certification.
2. Avoid penalty and be seen to be avoiding penalty.
3. Avoid reputational risk.
4. Continue to do business.

Sometimes people try to appeal to the purely altruistic to justify buying in to project cat foods. I think that's a big stretch. The official line goes, 'because we need to be good corporate citizens.' This one is problematic because 'the right thing' is highly subjective. Is it 'the right thing' according to the government? the regulator? the board? the executive? the operational team?

We're back to the different motivators between change initiators and change recipients. This gets overplayed. The ongoing business owner will need more than this to truly be motivated. Again, ask, 'If the regulatory piece doesn't go well, who will feel the pain the most and how?'

Identifying the business owner is half the battle. It's likely they still won't want to own a project cat foods. That's when influencing skills to get others onside need to come to the fore. Influencers at the same level as the target business owner are most useful for this, I've found. If you 'go above', it's too much like you 'dobbed them in for the short straw'. Go below and they've got no compelling reason to listen. They could even feel it's presumptuous. Someone at the same level they know and respect to make it 'just a friendly chat' is what's needed here. For these conversations, it matters where your senior responsible owner sits in the food chain and whether they're an effective influencer. Find a new ally if they're not. One with some clout.

When you do contract work over a prolonged period, you get to see a lot of business models in action. Often, the organisation's unifying purpose is not always reflected in the current organisational structure. In fact, most probably it's not. This makes things harder. It's always easier to find business owners in organisations that have a connection to their core purpose reflected in their organisational structure. That's when teams and business units are grouped logically around the work, its outputs, and its outcomes.

Here are a few examples of organisations I've worked in that have a clear line to their core purpose. It's easier to find a home for things when the structure and purpose of each 'room' in the building is clear.

1. Banks: 'We make money helping you to make the most out of your money.'

2. Police: 'We enforce the law to keep you safe from crime.'

3. Inland Revenue: 'We make sure you pay your taxes to fund society. We also penalise you when you don't pay.'

4. Accident Compensation Corporation: 'We help you when you hurt yourself.'

Of course, these are massive simplifications of complex organisations. However, if you can't encapsulate the core purpose of what an organisation does in these succinct statements, it's a sure bet that finding business owners will be harder.

You may deliver change in what I call a 'cluster' organisation. These are organisations that serve many purposes. Many government and federal agencies are cluster organisations. Successful identification of the right business owner is complex in a cluster organisation. It often takes a lot longer. It's particularly hard to find the business owner of the sustained change value. If you can't even work out how the pieces fit together, or why they're even grouped the way they are, it's very hard to see who should own what. Ownership of tactical 'widget' pieces is a lot easier, for example, when the learning team owns all the learning, the HR team owns the induction collateral, and so on.

Most organisations of any size have legacy pockets of people. They are disconnected from their 'home' function. This happens when managers functioning from tier three to tier five level make decisions about how to organise their patch. Each time this happens, a subunit or team within the business unit gets restructured. The logic the manager uses to restructure is often completely different from the original logic that set the business unit up. This gets compounded over many years and many managers. This means teams get disconnected from the wider business unit structures. The structural integrity of the business unit purpose starts to degrade. It pays to think very carefully through business ownership in these 'messy' legacy models. The most obvious business owner isn't always the right business owner.

Organisations also restructure at the enterprise level. For most of a decade, I worked for New Zealand's national telecommunications carrier. I saw a constant expansion and contraction around the four key dimensions that organisations can play with:

1. Functional orientation (vertical alignment): All the HR people are together, all the finance people together, all the product owners together, and so on.
2. Line of business orientation (horizontal alignment): All the people who work to provide the good or service are grouped together.
3. Centralised model: Decision-making is held at the centre in a head office.
4. Dispersed model: Decision-making is regionally dispersed.

Some other trends I've observed are as follows.

1. Management Issue: Concerned that customer service and product and/or service delivery aren't responsive enough to customer needs.

   Solution: Move to 'line of business orientation' (horizontal alignment). The strategy is that if you move all the contributors in the value chain closer to the customer, they're also closer to the consequence of nondelivery and/or inferior products and service. Meaning that they'll care more and lift their game.

2. Management Issue: Concerned that capability is low and/or too dispersed.

   Solution: Move to 'functional orientation' (vertical alignment). And so the cycle continues.

These are key movements I've seen during my career. It's likely that in the delivery cycle of your project, you'll see some of these patterns. You need to be savvy about where the trend is heading. Pin your business ownership to where the trend is going, not where it came from.

These movements are a real challenge to manage. That's along with fending off the owners of the tactical artefacts from attempts to own the realised change value. There's a useful shortcut if you have a functional oriented organisational model. If you have this, then operations are often a sure bet for ownership of realised value. That's because they're closer to the pointy end of the outcome.

Summary

That's the end of chapter 10, the final chapter. This chapter covers how to ensure you identify the correct business owners. It describes the difference between tactical business ownership of artefacts and strategic business ownership of the realised change value (outcomes and benefits). It explores the difference between functional output owners and outcome owners, and it explains outcomes that are achieved when the change value is realised. It emphasises the importance of starting the search for business owners early. It covers the top four dimensions of organisational restructure, and how to work out where your organisation is in the cycle of these structural changes. Land the business ownership in the structure the organisation is moving toward, not where it came from.

Conclusion

That's the end of this book and our adventure together, at least for now. I hope you find something helpful in it to carry with you into your next change management assignment.

Remember you can download a free copy of the workbook to use on the job in conjunction with this book at www.barbgrant.com/changethatsticksworkbook.

Here you can sign up to stay connected with me and my ongoing work. There are so many other topics to be covered, such as how to manage successful enterprise change and how to deliver change management on large-scale transformation programmes.

If you found something of value in this book then please let me know what you liked. Also send me your feedback if you think there's something that could be improved or added! I'd love to hear from and yes—it'll be me who responds—my only minion at this stage is Change Cat!

If you did get some value from reading *Change Management that Sticks*, I would be grateful if would please leave me a 5-star review on Amazon and write some thoughts on what you liked best about it. That would be an immense help. Thanks!

You can also connect with me on LinkedIn at www.linkedin.com/in/barbgrantcoach/. I'm very active on there and would love to engage.

Let the practical tips and templates in this book now be a companion to you on your journey to change management that sticks. My fellow change manager, I salute you!

Abbreviations in Change Management

BAU Business as Usual: Things being run within the normal operation of the business rather than set up as a separate project initiative.

CapEx: Capital Expenditure. Major long-term expenses.

CE: Chief Executive. Tier one leader in an organisation. Usually the leader of a public sector organisation is a CE.

CEO: Chief Executive Officer. Tier one leader in an organisation. Usually the leader of a private sector organisation is a CEO.

CFO: Chief Financial Officer. The head of the finance function in an organisation. Usually the CFO is a direct report to the tier one leader.

HR: Human Resources. The function in an organisation that manages people. Key activities within the HR function are usually recruitment, payroll, employee relations, remuneration, talent acquisition and management, business advisory (on people-related issues).

IT: Information Technology. The function in an organisation that manages technology.

KPIs: Key Performance Indicators. A quantifiable measure used to evaluate the success of an organization, employee, and so on in meeting objectives for performance.

OpEx: Operational Expenditure. Day-to-day expenses.

ROI: Return on Investment. A calculation of the monetary value of an investment versus its cost. The ROI formula is 'profit minus cost'.

UAT: User Acceptance Testing. A phase of software development in which the software is tested in the real world by its intended audience.

WIIFM: What's in it for me? The positives delivered by a change initiative that will motivate a person to adopt the change.

Endnotes

Chapter 1

1. IBM Global Business Services, n.d. 'Making change work … while the work keeps changing. How change architects lead and manage organizational change,' *IBM*. 14 August 2014. www.ibm.com/downloads/cas/WA3NR3NM.

2. 'Person in the arena' from the introduction of this book. A reference to the 'Man in the Arena' speech about Theodore Roosevelt. (Theodore Roosevelt Center: Dickinson State University, North Dakota, n.d.) Accessed 3 October 2020. www.theodorerooseveltcenter.org/Learn-About-TR/TR-Encyclopedia/Culture-and-Society/Man-in-the-Arena.aspx.

3. See website of Susan David, PhD at www.susandavid.com, n.d. Accessed 24 October 2019. See also 'Six Seconds: The emotional intelligence network' at www.6seconds.org.

Chapter 3

4. IBM Global Business Services, n.d. 'Making change work … while the work keeps changing. How change architects lead and manage organizational change,' *IBM*. Accessed 14 August 2014. www.ibm.com/downloads/cas/WA3NR3NM.

Chapter 4

5. Spinify. 'The Positive Effect of Negative Incentives', accessed 20 April 2017. https://spinify.com/blog/positive-effect-negative-incentives/.

6. Greg Johanson. '"Taking over" technique with veteran trauma work.' Accessed 18 September 2022. https://hakomiinstitute.com/Resources/Johanson-TakingOverwVets.pdf.

7. Quote Investigator, n.d. 'The test of a first-rate intelligence is the ability to hold two opposed ideas in the mind at the same time.' Accessed 16 October 2022. https://quoteinvestigator. com/2020/01/05/intelligence/.

Chapter 5

8. Tim Creasey. n.d. 'Defining Change Impact.' *Prosci.* Accessed 16 October 2022. www.prosci.com/resources/articles/ defining-change-impact

Chapter 6

9. Research shows it takes six seconds to move emotions. See 'Six Seconds: The Emotional Intelligence Network' at www.6seconds.org. Accessed 24 October 2019.

10. The University of Texas Permian Basin. n.d. 'How much of communication is nonverbal?' Accessed 21 November 2022. https://online.utpb.edu/about-us/articles/communication/ how-much-of-communication-is-nonverbal/.

Chapter 7

11. RTT, Rapid Transformational Therapy, n.d. See at https://rtt. com. Accessed 20 November 2022

Chapter 8

12. W. B. Yeats. 'The second coming.' 'A gaze blank and pitiless as the sun' is a line in this poem. Poetry Foundation, n.d. Accessed 15 October 2022.

13. Wayne Huang, John Mitchell, Carmel Dibner, Andrea Ruttenberg, and Audrey Tripp. 16 January 2018. 'How customer service can turn angry customers into loyal ones.' Harvard Business Review. https://hbr.org/2018/01/

how-customer-service-can-turn-angry-customers-into-loyal-ones.

Chapter 9

14. Here are some word cloud generators:

    - https://monkeylearn.com/word-cloud
    - Digi Poll Apps
    - https://doodle.com/poll-maker. This one says, 'Free and easy to use poll maker from Doodle! Sign up now!" n.d. Accessed 18 September 2022.
    - www.mentimeter.com/features/live-polling for 'Live polling tool' by Mentimeter, n.d. Accessed 20 November 2022.

15. Instructional Design Junction, n.d. 'The 7 plus or minus 2 rule and the chunking principle'. Accessed 18 September 2022. https://instructionaldesignjunction.com/2021/08/23/george-a-millers-7-plus-or-minus-2-rule-and-simon-and-chases-chunking-principle/.

16. Swetha Venkataramani, 13 May 2021. 'Make way for a more human-centric employee value proposition.' *Gartner.* www.gartner.com/smarterwithgartner/make-way-for-a-more-human-centric-employee-value-proposition.

17. Chris Brown, 9 November 2021. '140 Emails per day over a year equivalent to using 16,800 plastic bags.' HRD, TheHRDIRECTOR. www.thehrdirector.com/business-news/csr-3/140-emails-per-day-over-a-year-equivalent-to-using-16800-plastic-bags/.

18. Robert S. Kaplan and David P. Norton, January-February 1992. 'The balanced scorecard—measures that drive performance.' Harvard Business Review. https://hbr.org/1992/01/the-balanced-scorecard-measures-that-drive-performance-2.

Glossary of Terms

There's a lot of love in my family for words. I also love pop culture and I love playfulness. Playfulness is a major theme in the book—that's why it features Change Cat. As stated in the introduction, this book is a conversation. So there's a lot of slang and a lot of pop culture references. I have a weakness for puns and side references. It keeps me amused, hopefully you too and makes the work (and the read) easier and more fun.

When my husband read this as a draft, he commented on the number of these slang expressions and pop culture references. He suggested a glossary of terms would be useful to keep readers in the loop. Therefore, please find below a chapter-by-chapter glossary of the terms, expressions, and pop culture references used throughout. I provide them in the order you will read them.

Introduction

wheelhouse: one's area of speciality or expertise.

Chapter 1

business change: when an organisation improves, restructures, or transforms a major part of its operations, disrupting systems, people, and processes.

cognitive dissonance: the state of having inconsistent thoughts, beliefs, or attitudes, especially as relating to behavioural decisions and attitude change.

uncanny valley: the phenomenon whereby a computer-generated figure of a humanoid robot bearing a near-identical resemblance to a human being arouses a sense of unease or revulsion in the person viewing it. Here used to refer to a sense of displacement and general unease with a business change one is supposed to sell to users, but to which one feels no personal values alignment.

professional burnout: a special type of work-related stress. A state of physical or emotional exhaustion that also involves a sense of reduced accomplishment and loss of personal identity.

talk myself 'off the ledge': to relieve someone's pain, worries, or concerns after they have experienced a difficult situation.

organisational culture knew: the collective knowledge of all individuals who make up an organisation. Based on the values, expectations, and practices that guide and inform the actions of all team members.

change enabler: someone who empowers a change to happen.

heads up: a message that alerts or prepares.

stick their head above the parapet: to do or say something that one thinks is important even though it may be perceived negatively.

running on empty: having almost reached a point where you are unable to continue, because you have almost no energy.

personal touchstone: a personal symbol or emblem that represents your dream and helps you to stay on track and true to your vision.

the grass is always browner: a paraphrase of the idiom 'The grass is always greener on the other side of the fence.' Here to indicate that no situation is ever perfect.

it's legit: conforming to the rules, authentic.

draw from a dry well: try to take from a source that is empty.

certain doggedness: a stubborn refusal to give in.

still the go: something still remains the right thing to do.

playing in the sandpit: all those working in an interaction.

Chapter 2

stakeholder: a person or group with an interest or concern in something.

these players: the people involved in the change

tsunami wave of issues: a build-up of objections and barrier to change taking place.

all the classics: here used to mean all the standard reasons why a stakeholder in a change process feels their needs have not been anticipated or met.

change actor: a person or group involved in a change process.

for the long haul: to be willing to be involved in an activity or situation for a long time, until it gets completed.

turned toward the change: how a stakeholder orients to a change. This refers to what attracts them to a change and what repulses them.

servant leader: a leadership philosophy built on the belief that the most effective leaders strive to serve others, rather than accrue power or take control.

live in the wild: in a free and natural state.

caught a unicorn: capturing something that is highly desirable but difficult to find or obtain.

scope creep: a sudden increase to the scope of a project.

fat stack of cash: a huge amount of money. As per Jesse in the series *Breaking Bad*.

stakeholder assessment: an analysis that identifies those people and groups involved in a business change and groups them according to their relationship to what is delivered and their attitude to it.

taken as gospel: believed to be true

stakeholder landscape: a relational view of all the stakeholders involved in a business change.

sense-making: the action or process of making sense of or giving meaning to something, especially new developments and experiences.

playback tool: a way of re-running what has happened to validate common understanding.

who's playing: those involved in a change process in the four stakeholder groups: initiators, partners, recipients, and onlookers.

derail your go-live: obstruct the implementation process.

go-live: the date on which a business change is launched to the recipients.

on to it: a person who knows what is going on.

roadblocks: barriers to business change implementation and adoption.

cut corners: to do something in the easiest, cheapest, or fastest way.

live in an ivory tower: to be disconnected from the reality of a situation.

generalist: a person whose skills and abilities are varied or unspecialised.

the edges of scope: to define the boundaries of something (so as to be capable of explaining it to another) i.e., 'the change means xxxx will happen, but xxxx will stay the same.'

change journey: the process of moving from a current state to a future state.

Chapter 3

sad face moment: emoji face used when pleading or when trying to win compassion or sympathy.

sleight of hand: dexterity in performing conjuring tricks; a poker analogy

plays out: develops or ends in a particular way.

Rubik's Cube: a puzzle consisting of a cube of six colours, each face of which is made up of nine squares, eight of which are individually rotatable. The aim is to swivel the squares until each face of the cube shows one colour only.

eye bouncing off the change: an analogy indicating that people want to see or buy in to a change (if there is no personal appeal that matters to them).

sell the sizzle: the original phrase is 'Sell the sizzle, not the steak.' Meaning that you should sell the benefits instead of the features, or sell people what they want, not what they need.

lay the bread crumb trail: from the fairy tale of Hansel and Gretel. The children break off pieces of bread to leave a trail they can follow to get them back home.

winky face: emoji used to indicate a playful joke.

subvert the dominant paradigm: phrase used to mean changing or overthrowing the current most prevalent set of beliefs.

toe the party line: to do what someone in authority tells you to do although you may not agree with it.

the emperor's new clothes: from the fairy tale. Something widely accepted as true or professed as being praiseworthy, due to an unwillingness of the general population to criticise it or be seen as going against popular opinion.

heart of change: a phrase underscoring the need to identify the emotional appeal of the change for each recipient to increase the chance of adoption.

force will not be with you: a Star Wars reference, it is a paraphrase of 'May the force be with you' used to wish an individual or group good luck or good will.

prefrontal cortex saddles up the amygdala and rides it back to the corral: analogy indicating that the higher reasoning centre of the brain (prefrontal cortex) rather than the emotional trigger centre (amygdala) must be in control to avoid a strong reaction to a newly introduced change.

a policy wonk: a person who studies or develops strategies and policies, sometimes in isolation from where the strategies and policies are used. That person, therefore, runs the risk of being too theoretical and lacking practicality.

field of dreams syndrome: movie reference to *Field of Dreams*. The idea that in business 'If you build it, they will come' as a false assumption that something will 'change the world' just by doing it.

Chapter 4

change impact assessment: document that defines how changes affect target audiences as they transition from the current to future state.

one ring to rule them all: a reference to the Lord of the Rings series. Here used to mean the central piece (change document) that brings everything together.

gap statement: an expression of what the difference between how something is currently done and how it will be done in a future state.

single source of truth: a central repository of information carrying credibility that its contents are up-to-date and valid.

traceability: the ability to track something through a process to understand where it originated, how it has evolved, and who made the decisions relating to it.

slice and dice: structure the information in small pieces.

to cut to the chase: to get to the point.

nosedived: a fast and sudden fall to the ground with the front pointing down. Most commonly referred to a plane crash.

corporate speak: jargon used which is specific to the large corporations, bureaucracies, and similar workplaces where it is used.

culture sucks: an organisation that lacks psychological safety. Therefore, employees are not free to say what they really think and feel.

project cat foods: regulatory projects. A thing that must be had but isn't desirable.

don't try to blag it: do not try to persuade others through guile.

doddle: a very easy task.

pull a swifty: to intentionally deceive another person. Also a reference to 'Rick and Morty' as in 'Get Swchifty', season two, episode five.

shakin' hands and kissin' babies: a practice in which politicians and candidates campaigning for office shake hands and kiss babies in order to garner public support.

does what it says on the tin: does exactly what it is intended to do.

if it's a dog: phrase meaning something unpleasant or boring.

lipstick the pig: make superficial changes to something generally regarded with dislike or disfavour in a fruitless attempt to make it more appealing.

fight the law but the law won: here used to mean you can't fight the inexorable. Song lyric by 'The Clash'

blow-back: negative reactions or results that were not intended, such as criticism, protest, or anger.

fist pump: celebratory gesture in which the fist is raised in front of the body and then quickly and vigorously drawn back.

worth it in spades: as valuable as the highest suit in the game bridge, which is spades.

level the perception: here used to mean finding the balance between extreme perceptions of the impact of a change. Finding the point that most accurately reflects how big the impact of change really is.

keep the change honest: ensure that the perception of the scale of change is kept as accurate as possible by hearing competing views on the subject.

agency and/or sovereignty: autonomy. Self-actualisation. The right to choose for oneself.

playing nice: behaving with others in a way that refrains from instigating trouble but hides one's real views.

rear an ugly head: something bad appears and causes troubles usually after not occurring for a period of time.

Chapter 5

guts of the approach: the core essentials.

so hot right now: the thing of the moment that everyone desire. *Zoolander* quote.

mate of mine: a friend.

growing edge of possibility: at the place that embraces innovation.

sussing things out: to find or discover.

be a bit stealthy about it: be deliberate and a bit secretive in how one goes about something.

unconscious bias: social stereotypes about certain groups of people that individuals form outside their own conscious awareness.

gung-ho: extremely or overtly zealous or enthusiastic.

on the fly: done quickly, without too much preparation.

postage stamp methods: something done easily without overly complicating activities.

temperature check: asking a question to benchmark where the respondents attitude currently sits.

stakeholder heat map: a quadrant used to identify stakeholders and categorise them in terms of their **influence** on a business change and the **impact** the business change will have on those stakeholders.

PowerPoint: slide show presentation programme.

WIIFM bank: A list of all the What's in it for me? (WIIFM) statements from which the items most appealing to a specific stakeholder group can be selected.

roll it up: collate information and express it at a more summarised level.

devolve back to legacy state: revert to how things used to be done before the change happened.

embed and sustain approach: a plan of action, consisting of a variety of interventions to ensure a business change endures and becomes second nature to the users.

ride or die artefacts: the artefacts you cannot miss out.

nitty gritty: the fine detail.

lost in the woods and can't see the trees: paraphrase of can't see the wood for the trees. Meaning on a business change project that the team becomes so lost in the details they can't see the big picture or the change story anymore.

as you do: as it is done.

a few issues: understated way of indicating there are challenges to something.

falling about and gnashing of teeth: being caught up in the drama of a challenge to the point that a rational solution cannot be discovered.

they railed: they complained.

drinking the Kool-Aid: a person or group who believe in a possibly doomed, dangerous and or erroneous idea due to the group reinforcing its own thinking and the pressure to conform. Originated from the Jim Jones mass suicide.

lotus eater: existing in a state of languorous indifference. Originally from *The Odyssey*, when Odysseus meets a group who eat the fruit of the legendary lotus. They lead a life of dreamy, indolent ease, indifferent to the busy world, lost in daydreams.

throw out the baby with the bath water: expression for an avoidable error in which something good is eliminated when trying to get rid of something bad.

resistance is futile: there is no point in showing opposition. Catch phrase of the Borg in Star Trek: The Next Generation. The Borg were an amalgamated race of biomechanical beings determined to assimilate every group of humans it encountered. If the targeted population refused to be assimilated, they were simply destroyed and the Borg moved on to its next target.

without a whimper, let alone a bang: paraphrase of the last two lines from T S Eliot's 1925 poem 'The hollow men': This is the way the world ends | Not with a bang but a whimper. Meaning that something is less exciting than what was expected or intended.

the lesser of two evils: the somewhat less unpleasant of two poor choices.

agile: iterative software-development methodology. Development and delivery happen via incremental sprint cycles. Things are delivered in chunks as they are developed.

waterfall approach: a linear project management approach whereby requirements are gathered at the beginning of a project and delivery happens when everything has been developed and tested. Everything is delivered all at once when completely finalised.

wagile: projects in which software is developed using an agile approach, but delivery uses a traditional waterfall approach.

going gangbusters: going strongly and doing well.

peg out: map out the structure of something and define its key points.

walk a mile in the recipient's shoes: a reminder to practice empathy. To understand your change recipients, you must understand their experiences, challenges, feelings, and thought processes.

Chapter 6

all the things: that which is currently fashionable or trendy. That which is currently given attention.

an empath: a person with the ability to perceive the mental and emotional state of another.

even a thing: used to question the validity of some trend, activity or pursuit.

big love fest: an event characterised by people's mutual appreciation or admiration of each other.

feeling of the pain: to suffer or have a disadvantage as a result of something.

an end in itself: something done because one wants to and not because it will help achieve or accomplish something else.

turned up the dial: increased the intensity of something.

the way: the rules and creed of how to behave. From the series, The Mandalorian.

like hires like: due to unconscious and conscious bias, people tend to hire more people like themselves because that's who they're comfortable with.

gets a whiff: receive a strong and intense awareness of something.

ducks were in a row: activities organised so that you're ready for the next step.

pulsating emotional sponge: a person demonstrating so much empathy that they are sucking up the feelings of everyone around them. This makes them overemotional and less analytical and rational.

the custodian of all things emotional and icky: situation where one person is made in charge of dealing with everyone else's emotions.

talking the talk but not walking the walk: hypocrisy, where there is a gap between how you say you want others to behave and how you act yourself.

keyboard warrior: a person who posts highly opinionated messages online in an aggressive or abusive manner, often without revealing their identity.

presenteeism: the lost productivity when employees are present at work but not working to the fullness of their abilities.

best of British: UK expression of encouragement. Pride in something being British in origin.

good fit: to be perfect to meet the requirements of a role.

hard-eyed: a shrewd person most focussed on financial return.

house wins: casinos are geared so that the house (meaning the casino) always make a net profit. The odds are stacked.

average man on the street: the ordinary person.

bread and butter: the core activity that keeps you going.

blue blood: membership in a noble or socially prominent family.

old Etonian: a former student of Eton College, a famous and expensive private school in England usually attended by the top social class.

played the odds: to act, hoping for a particular outcome.

deep end of opportunity: furthest end in a range of choices, where there is more upside but also more downside.

hire pool: the group of candidates available for a role.

couldn't fathom: can't understand

pored through the manual: read the manual with great concentration.

had the bottle: had the courage.

finicky: fastidious and fussy.

new-fangled: the most recent style.

walk-throughs: stepping through a sequence in order to check whether it is correct and commonly understood.

Toto, we're not in Kansas anymore: quote from *The Wizard of Oz*. Realising you aren't where you thought you were anymore.

all the rage: very popular at a certain time.

the road is long and full of challenges: a demanding course of action to take. Also a paraphrase of the quote 'the night is long and full of terrors' from *Game of Thrones*.

capability building: developing skills and knowledge required to complete tasks.

capability gap: difference between the skills and competencies employees have now and the ones they need in the future.

shot themselves in the foot: sabotaged their own efforts.

hot spots: the things that are changing that will get the strongest reaction.

who calls the shots on who: who gets to decide what others do.

leadership advocacy: those accountable for the change take positive continuous action to support the desired outcomes.

champion: someone who advocates for a business change.

champion networks: a group of employees nominated and tasked with supporting a business change to increase buy-in and adoption.

influencer pool: the group of people who the change recipients really listen to. Not necessarily leaders or managers.

backfill: put another person into a role so that the original person is freed up from their normal workload.

end-to-end pilot: a test of the change run in controlled conditions, starting with the first thing that is changing and ending with the last. Validates that everything is ready for the change to be delivered to all recipients.

stagger the roll-out: deliver the group to one area and/or group before another receives it, at spaced out intervals.

adopt an adaptive mindset: to take on a pliable attitude that can embrace and adapt to new circumstances. See Carol S. Dweck's book, *Mindset: The New Psychology of Success.*

on the fritz: has an error

glaring typo: obvious type-set mistake

Magic 8-Ball: plastic sphere used for fortune-telling or to seek advice.

whack: hit

fight or flight: the instinctive physiological response to a threatening situation that readies one either to resist forcibly or to run away.

attrition rates: metric used to measure employees lost over a period of time.

Chapter 7

creative struggle: an exploration of possibility via the exploration of conflict and resolution. See the psychotherapy known as Hakomi.

trust issues: fear of betrayal, abandonment, or manipulation.

dob them in: to tell somebody about something that another person has done wrong.

spidey senses: to have a feeling or intuition about something, like Spider-Man does.

tight with the people: have a close relationship with the people being discussed.

save face: avoid having someone lose respect for themself.

keep the wheels on: help something to continue and thereby avoid a crash.

won the battle but lost the war: military analogy meaning to achieve a minor victory that ultimately leads to a larger defeat.

bite down: refuse to let something go.

keepin' it real: to remain honest, genuine, and authentic. To be true to oneself.

glossing over: avoiding the hard issues.

intel: useful information on a subject of interest.

what have I got to lose: a question to ask in a situation that could improve by doing something and that won't be any worse if it fails.

I'm outta here: I'm leaving.

voice of the change: what people really think and feel about a change, but maybe don't say overtly.

know where the bodies are buried: a person with a long institutional history of an organisation knows all the rumours and secrets.

quid pro quo: a favour for a favour, this for that. I'll scratch your back if you scratch mine.

heart of the issue: the most important aspect.

Chapter 8

rock the crunchy stuff: rise up to do the difficult challenges and handle them well.

get ugly early: communicate bad news quickly.

jewel in the crown: something that is the most valuable, important, or admired of its kind.

save face: to behave so as to avoid having other people losing respect for oneself.

bleeding obvious: a thing so apparent it doesn't need to be stated.

play your audience for a fool: treat people like they're stupid.

spin doctoring: dressing a situation up to sound better than it really is.

tenacious in a fight: resilient when challenged.

downstream consequences: negative things that will happen after something else has happened in a chain reaction.

skew the pitch: to twist or distort.

facing into: taking on a difficult challenge directly.

curly things: difficult and complex challenges.

jam at the same joints: seen together.

pad out: making something bigger than it actually is

pet peeve: a thing that personally annoys a lot.

Oompa Loompas: short, orange-skinned workers at the chocolate factory in the movie, *Willy Wonka & the Chocolate Factory* by Roald Dahl.

food and rations: the necessaries of being employed and managed in an organisation.

kick the can down the road: deferring dealing with something until a later date.

ear to the ground: listening intently to the overt and covert signals being sent.

watershed moment: a point of significant transition.

sh!t just got real: the moment that a thing moves from potential to actual.

life's rich tapestry: difficult or bad experiences that are part of a full and interesting life.

spook the horses: to scare or cause an upset.

point forward to the North Star: reiterate the vision and outcomes.

seeding: planting an idea early for later discussion.

fait accompli: something that is finished and the outcome is irreversible.

shell game: a trick used to indicate that something is happening whereas something else is really going on.

back at the ranch: what is happening in another place at the same time.

in the project tent: inside the project team.

litmus test: a decisively indicative test.

crunchiest news: hardest messages.

Chapter 9

seat of the pants: employing knowledge gained through personal experience, judgement, and effort rather than technological aids or formal theory.

got a feel for: to begin to understand how to do something well.

change fatigue: recipients' exhaustion with continuous change.

funky apps: modern applications.

digital poll: an electronic poll run online.

word cloud: a visual representation of word data. That is, a collection or cluster of words depicted in different sizes. The bigger and bolder the word, the more often it is mentioned in a given text or transcribed from free text written by respondents.

skin in the game: a stake in what's happening.

middle-of-the-road: standing for or following a course of action midway between extremes.

meh: expressing a lack of interest or enthusiasm.

grip up: to commit to undertake something. To get hold of something.

culture is watching: organisational culture observes everything that happens in the environment and draws conclusions on what behaviour is okay and not okay based on this.

calling card: an indicator of what can be expected.

complicater: person or people making things more complicated.

p!ssing contest: a competition between rivals to determine superiority, predominance, or leadership.

all the users to the yard: a paraphrase of the song lyric by Kelis, 'My milkshake brings all the boys to the yard.'

drinks too much of its own Kool-Aid: in love with its own rhetoric. A person or group who believe in a possibly doomed, dangerous, and/or erroneous idea due to the group reinforcing its own thinking and the pressure to conform. Originated from the Jim Jones mass suicide.

starting gate: a barrier used to start a race.

point of difference: thing that makes something unique.

prepped: prepared.

uptake: level of usage by how many people.

mop-up session: events run to pick up change recipients who couldn't attend the ones held previously.

daily go-live triage model: the approach used to determine the priority of incidents encountered when a project goes live and to assign the incidents to the correct owner to fix them.

problem child: a child who is particularly difficult to raise or educate.

runs on the board: achieves some goals.

old school measures: approaches developed some time ago that may have fallen out of favour.

flapping in the breeze: something that is exposed and therefore vulnerable.

a through-line: something that shows a clear relationship between one thing and another.

Chapter 10

'Hot Potato': song sung by the Australian child entertainment group, The Wiggles. Here it refers to prospective business owners attempting to pass ownership of what a project delivers as though it were a hot potato.

empire builders: managers intent on gaining power and status for themselves.

land grab: a usually swift acquisition of land or, in this case, team-members, roles, and potential functions in an organisational structure.

prime the pump: prepare for what's coming

SteerCo: the project steering committee. The group that performs the governance function on a project.

sightline to early pipeline issues: view of upcoming work and related issues.

canary in the coal mine: something whose sensitivity to adverse conditions makes it a useful early indicator of such conditions.

get it in the neck: be punished or criticised.

dobbed them in: told on someone.

the short straw: the least enjoyable thing of a range of duties, because you have been chosen to do it.

clout: status, power.

tier three to tier five level managers: managers in an organisation who sit from the third to fifth level in the hierarchy.

Accident Compensation Corporation: a public sector organisation in New Zealand that provides comprehensive, no-fault personal injury cover for all New Zealand residents and visitors to New Zealand.

fending off: defend or protect from something.

pointy end: painful place where consequence and accountability are realised.

Acknowledgements

Thanks to my husband, Pete, who is, in all things, my greatest strength. Also to my children who make it worthwhile. The Change Cat illustrations are my creation, but my daughter's talents brought them to life. Grateful thanks to Paige for lending her never-ending flare for the whimsical to Change Cat. Paige did all of these illustration whilst studying for Year 13 exams, so thanks for bearing with this during demanding times. Also thanks to Dan who lent a skilled hand doing tricky things like cat paws holding canes and defining the perfect proportions of an elephant!

Enormous thanks to my early readers, Sue Morris, Natalie Thomson, Anne Rainey, and Karen Howarth. Your helpful but kind advice was invaluable and much appreciated.

There are many people who contributed to the thinking in this book and lent a colourful turn of phrase that has stayed with me since our adventures together and made it into this book. Special shout out to Bronnie, Morgan, Stu, Marc, Bridgit, and Mel for a particularly spicy turn of phrase.

Thanks to my proof-reader Susan Keillor and my editor Nina Shoroplova for putting the final polish on it. Thanks to Geoff Affleck for supportive and much-needed advice on book publication, marketing, and launch.

Finally, thanks to all the people I've ever worked with to get a business change project delivered and make it stick. Your wisdom, humour, and tenacity helped show me how it's done and the resilience it takes to deliver change management if you really care about outcome. This book is in part my dedication to you and to the reader who will continue, in service, to the art of change management.

Author Bio

Barb Grant is a business change manager with a thirty-year proven track record in successful change management delivery. Her mission is to teach others how to deliver business change that makes organisations more effective, profitable, and successful, and yet never loses sight of the fact that organisations are made up of people. Barb believes that project and change management methodologies must be the servant and not the master of the change practitioner. She believes in deep dialogue, emotional authenticity, playfulness, and a genuine people-centred approach. That's what you need to make sure your business change is actively used for great results and not just a dust gatherer.

Services

Barb Grant is a lead consultant delivering bold change management that sticks. At her website you can download a PDF workbook to use on-the-job in conjunction with this book.

Her range of services are listed on her website at barbgrant.com. Here are just a few of them:

- Strategic business change management consulting.
- Business change management delivery.
- Change management practice establishment.
- Mentoring and coaching of change management teams and practitioners.

Printed in Great Britain
by Amazon

40999327R00128